# GARDENER

# GROUNDS MAINTENANCE WORKER

Edited by

HY HAMMER

Chief of
Examining Service Division
New York City
Department of Personnel (Ret.)



AN ARCO BOOK

Published by Prentice Hall Press
New York, NY 10023

An Arco Book
Published by Prentice Hall Press
A Division of Simon & Schuster, Inc.
Gulf + Western Building
One Gulf + Western Plaza
New York, New York 10023



Manufactured in the United States of America

1 2 3 4 5 6 7 8 9 10

**Library of Congress Cataloging-in-Publication Data**

Gardener, grounds maintenance worker.

"An Arco book."
1. Landscape gardening—Examinations, questions, etc.
2. Civil service—New York (N.Y.)—Examinations.
I. Hammer, Hy.
SB469.6.G37 1986 635.9′076 86-12272
ISBN 0-668-06604-0

# CONTENTS

# WHAT THIS BOOK WILL DO FOR YOU

ARCO Publishing, Inc. has followed testing trends and methods ever since the firm was founded in 1937. We specialize in books that prepare people for tests. Based on this experience, we have prepared the best possible book to help *you* score high.

To write this book we carefully analyzed every detail surrounding the forthcoming examination . . .

- the job itself
- official and unofficial announcements concerning the examination
- all the previous examinations, many not available to the public
- related examinations
- technical literature that explains and forecasts the examination

## CAN YOU PREPARE YOURSELF FOR YOUR TEST?

You want to pass this test. That's why you bought this book. Used correctly, your "self-tutor" will show you what to expect and will give you a speedy brush-up on the subjects tested in your exam. Some of these are subjects not taught in schools at all. Even if your study time is very limited, you should:

- Become familiar with the type of examination you will have.
- Improve your general examination-taking skill.
- Improve your skill in analyzing and answering questions involving reasoning, judgment, comparison, and evaluation.
- Improve your speed and skill in reading and understanding what you read—an important part of your ability to learn and an important part of most tests.

This book will tell you exactly what to study by presenting in full every type of question you will get on the actual test.

This book will help you find your weaknesses. Once you know what subjects you're weak in you can get right to work and concentrate on those areas. This kind of selective study yields maximum test results.

This book will give you the *feel* of the exam. Almost all our sample and practice questions are taken from actual previous exams. On the day of the exam you'll see how closely this book follows the format of the real test.

This book will give you confidence *now,* while you are preparing for the test. It will build your self-confidence as you proceed and will prevent the kind of test anxiety that causes low test scores.

This book stresses the multiple-choice type of question because that's the kind you'll have on your test. You must not be satisfied with merely knowing the correct answer for each question. You must find out why the other choices are incorrect. This will help you remember a lot you thought you had forgotten.

After testing yourself, you may find that you are weak in a particular area. You should concentrate on improving your skills by using the specific practice sections in this book that apply to you.

# Part One

## *Applying and Studying for the Job*

# EXAMINATION ANNOUNCEMENT

**DUTIES AND RESPONSIBILITIES**

Under supervision, does gardening work; performs related work.

**EXAMPLES OF TYPICAL TASKS**

Plants, cultivates and cares for trees, flowers, plants, shrubs and other flora.

Digs up, balls, burlaps and transplants trees and shrubs. Digs up and transplants sod. Pots flowers and plants. Propagates plant life.

Prepares soil and seed beds. Grades, sods, weeds, mulches, and mows lawns. Repairs damaged planted areas. As necessary, fertilizes and waters soil, prunes and sprays trees, shrubs and plants.

Operates and cares for hand and power gardening tools and equipment and makes necessary operating adjustments to same; reports need for repairs and replacements.

As required, keeps simple records and makes written reports.

May supervise subordinate employees, including temporary workers, instructing them in gardening techniques and in the proper use and care of materials and equipment.

As directed, performs various tasks in connection with cleaning of grounds and painting of fixtures and equipment.

**QUALIFICATION REQUIREMENTS**

1. Two (2) years of full-time paid experience in gardening work, including experience in each of the following: planting, cultivating and caring for trees, plants, shrubs and lawns; or
2. Thirty credits in gardening, agriculture or a related field from an accredited college or community college, and one (1) year of experience as described above; or
3. A satisfactory equivalent combination of education and experience.

# TECHNIQUES OF STUDY AND TEST-TAKING

*Although a thorough knowledge of the subject matter is the most important factor in succeeding on your exam, the following suggestions could raise your score substantially. These few pointers will give you the strategy employed on tests by those who are most successful in this not-so-mysterious art. It's really quite simple. Do things right . . . right from the beginning. Make these successful methods a habit. Then you'll get the greatest dividends from the time you invest in this book.*

## PREPARING FOR THE EXAM

1. *Budget your time*. Set aside definite hours each day for concentrated study. Keep to your schedule.

2. *Study alone*. You will concentrate better when you work by yourself. Keep a list of questions you cannot answer and points you are unsure of to talk over with a friend who is preparing for the same exam. Plan to exchange ideas at a joint review session just before the test.

3. *Eliminate distractions*. Disturbances caused by family and neighbor activities (telephone calls, chit-chat, TV programs, etc.) work to your disadvantage. Study in a quiet, private room.

4. *Use the library*. Most colleges and universities have excellent library facilities. Some institutions have special libraries for the various subject areas: physics library, education library, psychology library, etc. Take full advantage of such valuable facilities. The library is free from those distractions that may inhibit your home study. Moreover, research in your subject area is more convenient in a library since it can provide more study material than you have at home.

5. *Answer all the questions in this book*. Don't be satisfied merely with the correct answer to each question. Do additional research on the other choices which are given. You will broaden your background and be more adequately prepared for

the "real" exam. It's quite possible that a question on the exam which you are going to take may require you to be familiar with the other choices.

6. *Get the "feel" of the exam.* The sample questions which this book contains will give you that "feel" since they are virtually the same as those you will find on the test.

7. *Take the Sample Tests as "real" tests.* With this attitude, you will derive greater benefit. Put yourself under strict examination conditions. Tolerate no interruptions while you are taking the sample tests. Work steadily. Do not spend too much time on any one question. If a question seems too difficult go to the next one. If time permits, go back to the omitted question.

8. *Tailor your study to the subject matter. Skim or scan.* Don't study everything in the same manner. Obviously, certain areas are more important than others.

9. *Organize yourself.* Make sure that your notes are in good order—valuable time is unnecessarily consumed when you can't find quickly what you are looking for.

10. *Keep physically fit.* You cannot retain information well when you are uncomfortable, headachy, or tense. Physical health promotes mental efficiency.

## HOW TO TAKE AN EXAM

1. *Get to the Examination Room about Ten Minutes Ahead of Time.* You'll get a better start when you are accustomed to the room. If the room is too cold, or too warm, or not well ventilated, call these conditions to the attention of the person in charge.

2. *Make Sure that You Read the Instructions Carefully.* In many cases, test-takers lose credits because they misread some important point in the given directions—example: the *incorrect* choice instead of the *correct* choice.

3. *Be Confident.* Statistics conclusively show that high scores are more likely when you are prepared. It is important to know that you are not expected to answer every question correctly. The questions usually have a range of difficulty and differentiate between several levels of skill.

4. *Skip Hard Questions and Go Back Later.* It is a good idea to make a mark on the question sheet next to all questions you cannot answer easily, and to go back to those questions later. First answer the questions you are sure about. Do not

panic if you cannot answer a question. Go on and answer the questions you know. Usually the easier questions are presented at the beginning of the exam and the questions become gradually more difficult.

If you do skip ahead on the exam, be sure to skip ahead also on your answer sheet. A good technique is periodically to check the number of the question on the answer sheet with the number of the question on the test. You should do this every time you decide to skip a question. If you fail to skip the corresponding answer blank for that question, all of your following answers will be wrong.

Each student is stronger in some areas than in others. No one is expected to know all the answers. Do not waste time agonizing over a difficult question because it may keep you from getting to other questions that you can answer correctly.

5. *Guess If You Are Not Sure.* No penalty is given for guessing when these exams are scored. Therefore, it is better to guess than to omit an answer.

6. *Mark the Answer Sheet Clearly.* When you take the examination, you will mark your answers to the multiple-choice questions on a separate answer sheet that will be given to you at the test center. If you have not worked with an answer sheet before, it is in your best interest to become familiar with the procedures involved. Remember, knowing the correct answer is not enough! If you do not mark the sheet correctly, so that it can be machine-scored, you will not get credit for your answers!

In addition to marking answers on the separate answer sheet, you will be asked to give your name and other information, including your social security number. As a precaution bring along your social security number for identification purposes.

Read the directions carefully and follow them exactly. If they ask you to print your name in the boxes provided, write only one letter in each box. If your name is longer than the number of boxes provided, omit the letters that do not fit. Remember, you are writing for a machine; it does not have judgment. It can only record the pencil marks you make on the answer sheet.

Use the answer sheet to record all your answers to questions. Each question, or item, has four or five answer choices labeled (A), (B), (C), (D), (E). You will be asked to choose the letter that stands for the best answer. Then you will be asked to mark your answer by blackening the appropriate space on your answer sheet. Be sure that each space you choose and blacken with your pencil is *completely* blackened. The machine will "read" your answers in terms of spaces blackened. Make sure that only one answer is clearly blackened. If you erase an answer, erase it completely and mark your new answer clearly. The machine will give credit only for clearly marked answers. It does not pause to decide whether you really meant (B) or (C).

Make sure that the number of the question you are being asked on the question sheet corresponds to the number of the question you are answering on the answer sheet. It is a good idea to check the numbers of questions and answers frequently. If you decide to skip a question, but fail to skip the corresponding answer blank for that question, all your answers after that will be wrong.

7. *Read Each Question Carefully*. The exam questions are not designed to trick you through misleading or ambiguous alternative choices. On the other hand, they are not all direct questions of factual information. Some are designed to elicit responses that reveal your ability to reason, or to interpret a fact or idea. It's up to you to read each question carefully, so you know what is being asked. The exam authors have tried to make the questions clear. Do not go astray looking for hidden meanings.

8. *Don't Answer Too Fast*. The multiple-choice questions which you will meet are not superficial exercises. They are designed to test not only your memory but also your understanding and insight. Do not place too much emphasis on speed. The time element is a factor, but it is not all-important. Accuracy should not be sacrificed for speed.

9. *Materials and Conduct at the Test Center*. You need to bring with you to the test center your Admission Form, your social security number, and several No. 2 pencils. Arrive on time as you may not be admitted after testing has begun. Instructions for taking the tests will be read to you by the test supervisor and time will be called when the test is over. If you have questions, you may ask them of the supervisor. Do not give or receive assistance while taking the exams. If you do, you will be asked to turn in all test materials and told to leave the room. You will not be permitted to return and your tests will not be scored.

# WORKING FOR THE CITY OF NEW YORK

## Where and How to Obtain Information

The New York City Department of Personnel—Recruitment Division can tell you about examinations scheduled to be held in the near future. Other sources of information include local newspapers such as the *Amsterdam News* or the weekly civil service newspaper, the *Chief-Leader* (sold at many newsstands or available at the library), the personnel offices of most city agencies, and the guidance or employment offices of local high schools, vocational institutions, and colleges. Professional associations have information regarding city positions in their professions, and community social agencies have such data as well.

The Applications Division of the New York City Department of Personnel can supply you with specific information about examinations currently open for filing. The division is located at 49 Thomas Street, New York, NY 10013. Filing is generally open only for twenty days during a month, and the actual examination is held two months later.

## Types of City Jobs

A wide variety of permanent competitive entrance-level civil service jobs are available in New York City government. You must meet the minimum qualifications for the job before taking an examination. If you pass the examination and are "reachable" on the list of eligible candidates, you may be hired. The minimum requirements are clearly stated in the Notice of Examination that is published for each examination. The majority of city jobs for which competitive examinations are given fall into one of the following categories:

**Professional** occupations require knowledge of a field of science or learning characteristically acquired through education or training equivalent to a bachelor's or higher degree with major study in or pertinent to the specialized field, as distinguished from general education (e.g., engineer, accountant, biologist, chemist).

**Technical/Semi-Professional** occupations are of two types. The first requires only college-level general education and/or equivalent experience related to the work being done (e.g., case worker, housing assistant, staff analyst). The second type involves work typically associated with and supportive of a professional administrative field, which is non-routine in nature (e.g., computer technician, electronic technician).

**Clerical** occupations involve structured work in support of office, business, or fiscal operations (e.g., clerk-typist, mail or file clerk). Many of these positions require no education or experience to be eligible to take the test.

**Uniformed** occupations include such positions in the police, fire, and corrections fields.

**Skilled Trades** include those positions requiring licenses and/or specific experience in a particular trade (e.g., carpenter, plumber).

**Unskilled/Labor** positions include those positions that require no formal education or experience, and a degree of heavy labor or physical activity is involved (e.g., park service worker, maintenance helper).

# How to Apply

When you know that you want to take a specific examination, you must obtain an application form and a Notice of Examination for the job you are seeking. Both of these are free of charge. For civil service positions that require experience and/or education, you must also fill out an Experience Paper—Form A. If your education was obtained outside the United States, an additional form (DP 398) must be completed. You can obtain all of the required forms from the application section of the New York City Department of Personnel during the filing period specified in the Notice of Examination, except on legal holidays and unless otherwise stated in the Notice.

After you have completed all the necessary forms, you may file them in person or by mail at the Application Division of the Department of Personnel. Mailed forms must be received by the last date for receipt of applications, as indicated in the Notice of Examination. You must include the filing fee with the completed forms. This amount is indicated on the Notice.

(Note: If you are receiving public assistance in New York City, the filing fee may not be required. You should file in person, *not* by mail, to obtain the waiver of the filing fee.)

# How to Fill Out the Application Form

The same simple application form is used for all New York City civil service examinations. Instructions for completing it are contained on the reverse side of the form.

## HOW TO FILL OUT EXPERIENCE PAPER—FORM A

The completion of Experience Paper—Form A is part of the examination for those positions that have minimum requirements. It is very important that you fill it out accurately and completely. Before you begin, be sure to read the Notice of Examination thoroughly to familiarize yourself with the specific minimum qualifications needed. Note whether there are any requirements that the candidate be a U.S. citizen and/or New York City resident. When filling out Experience Paper—Form A, follow these general instructions:

- Type, print, or write (in blue or black ink) the information requested.
- Be COMPLETE, CONCISE and ACCURATE. The information you enter is used to determine your rating on training and experience. If statements of material facts are found to be false, exaggerated, or misleading, you may be disqualified.
- DO NOT REVEAL YOUR IDENTITY in any way on this experience paper. If you are or have been in business for yourself or have been employed by a relative of the same name, write "self" or the relationship of the relative in the space headed "Name of Employer."

The following list will help you properly fill out each part of Experience Paper—Form A.

1. Begin by filling in your Social Security number (9 digits) in the box on the top right hand corner of the Experience Paper (e.g., 102/77/3456).
2. In the top middle of the Experience Paper, write the exact title of the examination you want to take. This information is given in the Notice of Examination.
3. Fill in the Examination Number (4 digits), given in the Notice of Examination, in the box in the top left-hand corner of the Experience Paper.
4. Do *not* fill in the boxes marked "Do Not Write in This Space."
5. **Box 1—License or Registration:** This data is required only if the Notice of Examination indicates that you have a license or registration in order to meet the qualification requirements. Positions requiring licenses or registrations include Chief Marine Engineer, for which you must have a valid license for Chief of Marine Vessels of a certain size to be qualified; or Inspector (Construction), for which you meet the minimum qualification requirements if you have a professional engineer's or architect's license pursuant to the New York State Education Law.

   To fill out Box 1, indicate in the specified places the title of the license or registration you possess, the License or Registration Number, the name of the issuing agency, the date it was originally issued to you, the date it was last renewed (or the Registration Renewal Number), and the date it expires.
6. **Box 2—Education:** In the appropriate spaces indicate the name of the last high school or trade/vocational school you attended, whether you went during the day or evening, the time you spent in that school (in months and years), whether or not you graduated, and the kind of diploma you received (academic, general, etc.).

   Note: If the requirements state that you may have a high school equivalency diploma instead of a high school diploma, give this information in this box.

   Give the same data for each college or other school you attended and also indicate the degree you received (if any), the total number of credits you completed, the major subject you studied, and the number of credits you earned in that major field. Do *not* submit a school transcript or diploma with your Experience Paper. In order to be qualified, your college must have been accredited by one of the accepted accrediting agencies. If you have doubts about this, check your local library or the school itself.

In addition, if you were educated in a country outside the United States, you must file Form DP 398, which you will receive with the Application Form and the Experience Paper—Form A. The DP 398 is used to evaluate foreign education in comparison to accredited educational institutions in the U.S.

7. **Box 3—Date of Birth:** The New York State Human Rights Law prohibits discrimination on the basis of age, but allows certain age specifications based on the duties of the individual title. If the Notice of Examination for the title you are seeking indicates age specifications based on bona fide occupational qualifications or on authorization in the law, you must indicate by giving your date of birth that you are within the limitations. For example, the title, Correction Officer, requires that (with certain exceptions for veterans) eligibles must have reached their 20th birthday by the date of appointment and must not have reached their 32nd birthday by the date of filing.

8. **Box 4:** In this box you are asked to indicate any courses you have passed which (a) are necessary to meet the minimum requirements for the position; (b) provide training appropriate to the position; or (c) are in related fields. This is especially important if you are looking for a position which requires college courses in a particular field. Suppose, for example, that your major was English Literature and that the minimum requirements for the job you seek is a number of credits in Sociology or Psychology. The Department of Personnel must have an indication that you possess these credits. In Box 4 indicate the name of the college or institution where you took each course, exact title of each course, course number, number of credits you received for each course, and date you completed each course. In listing the course title be sure to add a "G" to indicate if it was a graduate course.

9. The next section of the Experience Paper concerns the parts of your employment history which you feel qualify you for the position you want. In a separate box and in chronological order, list each job you believe qualifies you, starting with the most recent and working back to the first relevant employment. Use separate boxes for each change in duties with the same employer. If you were in the armed forces and had duties or training which help qualify you for the position you seek, list that in a separate box as well.

   Note: Make sure you read and understand the minimum requirements of the Notice of Examination, especially noting whether or not any required experience must have been on a *full-time paid* basis. If it does not, you should include any qualifying voluntary work that was not fragmentary or occasional in nature. Thus, if you served as a volunteer for 20 hours each week in the field, it may be credited toward meeting the minimum requirements, and so should be included unless the Notice of Examination states that work must have been full time and paid.

   When listing each work experience, include the dates of employment (give months and years), total length of employment, title of your position, both the starting and last salary, name and address of the firm where you worked, nature of the business, and number and titles of the workers you supervised. In addition, indicate the title (not the name) of your immediate supervisor, show whether or not the job was provisional in New York State or New York City government, and the number of hours you worked weekly.

Note: If you were self-employed or worked in a family firm where the name of the firm and/or your supervisor is the same as yours, do *not* indicate that name in the box, but write merely the relationship to the employer (e.g., under Name of Employer write "father's firm") and the address. This is essential in order to ensure complete impartiality.

10. You are now ready to describe your duties in that job. Be sure to describe your job in sufficient detail so that the Department of Personnel staff understands how those duties meet the requirements of the job you seek. For example, saying that you "helped budget your company's funds" does not tell whether you were a clerk, typist, bookkeeper, messenger, accountant, or analyst.

    Here is a sample of how you should describe each of the jobs you performed that you feel qualifies you for the position you seek.

| 1 Dates of Employment (give month and year) From 1/70 To 3/83 | Length of Employment Yrs. 13 Mos. 2 | Exact Title of Your Position STAFF ACCOUNTANT | Starting Salary $20,000 per YR. Last Salary $28,000 per YR. |
|---|---|---|---|
| Name and Address of Employer J. JONES CO. 138 BAKER ST CHICAGO, IL 19327 | | Nature of Employer's Business WHOLESALE JEWELRY | |
| | | Title (not name) of your Immediate Superior VICE PRESIDENT | |
| Number and Titles of Employees You Supervise 1 BOOKKEEPER | | If with New York City or State was this a provisional appointment? Yes ☐ No ☑ | No. of Hours Worked per Week 40 |

Describe Your Duties COMPLETELY IN CHARGE OF ALL PROFESSIONAL ACCOUNTING AND RELATED ACTIVITIES, INCLUDING PREPARATION OF TAX RETURNS, BUDGETING, SETTING UP BOOKS FOR PURCHASE AND SALES (AND AUDITING FOR ACCURACY), SALARY OF STAFF (100 PERSONS) ETC. PURCHASE = $2 MILLION PER YEAR. SALES = $6 MILLION PER YEAR.

11. **Other Experience:** In this box you should list other employment that you did not include in prior boxes. Indicate the dates of employment; the names, addresses, and types of businesses; titles you held; highest salary you were paid for each job; and a brief description of your work.

    In the last box of the Experience Paper, give additional qualifications which you think helps meet the necessary qualification requirements. List any article or pamphlet you have had published, or special certificate from professional boards you have earned. Remember not to mention your name in this area.

## Points to Remember

1. Before filing, make sure you carefully read and fully understand the minimum requirements and any medical and/or physical requirements given in the Notice of Examination. Be sure that you comply with any sex, age, citizenship, or residence requirements listed in the Notice. By doing this, you

are better able to determine if you are qualified. Remember that you will not receive a refund of your filing fee, and will not be placed on the list of eligibles, even if you pass the test, if you are found "Not Qualified."

2. After you have completed the Application Form, the Experience Paper, and any other papers required in the Notice of Examination, you must do either of the following:

   a. Hand deliver the material (or have it hand delivered) to the Applications Section of the Department of Personnel together with the filing fee (in cash or by check or money order payable to "The New York City Department of Personnel"); or
   b. Mail the material, together with a check or money order (*not* cash), payable to the Department of Personnel, in a stamped envelope to Applications Section, New York City Department of Personnel.

   All of the completed required forms and the filing fee must be received by the Department of Personnel by the last day for filing for the examination. The date of receipt, not date of postmark, is controlling.

3. Two weeks before the test you will receive an admission card to the test. This does not mean that the Department of Personnel has found that you meet the minimum requirements for the title, since in most cases your Experience Paper will be evaluated only after you have passed the test.

4. All information you list on the Experience Paper is subject to investigation by the Department of Personnel as to its truthfulness and accuracy. If investigation shows you do not meet the minimum requirements because the information given in the Experience Paper is untrue or unverifiable, you will be disqualified. If you are already on the job, you will be fired. The filing fee will not be returned to you. It is therefore very important that the information on your Experience Paper is accurate and verifiable.

5. The Experience Paper is part of the examination, and must contain no information that identifies you to the Department of Personnel's evaluation staff. Be sure that you do not put your name on any part of Experience Paper—Form A.

6. If there is insufficient room in any of the boxes on the Experience Paper, attach a separate piece of paper and use the same format to give the needed information. Do not put your name on this paper—just your Social Security number.

7. The tentative date of the first test in an examination is stated in the Notice of Examination. The official test date will be given on the admission card sent to you. If you do not receive an admission card within seven days prior to the tentative test, go to the Examining Service Division of the Department of Personnel during business hours to obtain an admission card.

8. Promptly notify in writing the Examining Service Division of any address change which occurs after filing the application and before you are notified of the test result. The Certification Division of the Department of Personnel must be notified, in writing, of any address change after notice-of-result cards are issued and during the life of an eligible list on which your name appears. Be sure to include your name, Social Security number, complete new address, title of examination, and examination number on all correspondence.

Failure to furnish such notification may result in the loss of opportunity to compete in tests, or to appear for appointment interviews.

## Special Assistance for the Physically Handicapped in Taking the Test

Examinations for entrance into the New York City Civil Service are generally written tests, and held in city public schools. As an Equal Opportunity Employer, the city encourages all qualified persons to compete for positions in government service. If you are physically handicapped, read the Notice of Examination you are interested in to determine whether or not medical or physical requirements exist that you cannot meet. If not, take the test. The Department of Personnel provides special assistance, including the services of an amanuensis and extra time to complete the exam, to candidates who are in wheelchairs or are physically unable to read and/or write because they are blind or have other disabling conditions.

## Provisions for Sabbath Observers or for Special Examination

1. Examinations for entrance into the New York City Civil Service are usually held on Saturdays. If you cannot take the test on that day because of bona fide religious reasons, the Department of Personnel will make special arrangements for you to take it on another day—generally on the Friday before the exam. Notify the Examining Service Division of the Department of Personnel of these reasons either in person or by registered or certified mail. You must present a signed statement from your religious leader certifying your religious beliefs. This must be received by the Department of Personnel not later than five days before the scheduled date of the examination.
2. The only reasons for the administration of a special examination on a date other than the one scheduled (other than noted above) are the following:
   a. The Department of Personnel made an error.
   b. You are compelled to go to court or appear before a public body or official that compels your appearance.
   c. You are employed by the city and were disabled during the course of your work, and are still disabled on the date of the test.
   d. The test is to be held within one week from the date of death of your spouse, mother, father, sister, brother, or child.

   If any of these occur, write to the Department of Personnel within two months after the exam date and submit written verification of the facts.
3. If you are taking an examination that has more than one test, and you have taken the first test but cannot take the next on the scheduled date because of military duty, apply to the Control and Service Division of the Department of Personnel with your separation papers not later than 90 days from termination of the military duty, and you will be given a special test at a later date.

# How to Do Well on the Competitive Tests

The competitive examination for most New York City Civil Service positions consists of one or more different types of tests, such as multiple choice, written essay, oral, practical, competitive physical, or a competitive rating of your education, training, and experience. In order to learn exactly what your examination will consist of, you must carefully read the Notice of Examination for the job you seek. The main part of this book will help you to get a high mark on the written tests. The Notice of Examination for the job you seek may also refer to a "selective certification" qualifying test. (See the Glossary at the end of this section to learn more about it.)

To be appointed to most city jobs, you do not have to take any medical or physical test, but some jobs do require a degree of physical work, such as lifting heavy objects or being able to climb or run, and so a qualifying test is given to those who have passed the competitive test. Again, read the Notice of Examination carefully to see that you are medically and physically able to meet these requirements.

All candidates for positions in New York City government must be able to understand and be understood in English. After you have passed the competitive tests and are called for possible appointment to a particular job, you may have to pass a simple qualifying test in order to prove that you understand and speak English.

# After the Tests Are Over

Follow any instructions that may be given to you on the last page of your test booklet. Then relax. You will be summoned for any additional tests, the eligible list will be established, and you will be advised of your test results. Final key answers will be published at the time the list is established. If you meet the minimum requirements as stated on the Examination Announcement, your name will be certified for appointment in due time. Be sure to notify the Certification Division of the Department of Personnel of any change of address. All eligible lists are subject to investigation, and if you are summoned for that process, bring with you all required documents. You have two months from the date of establishment of the eligible list to file an appeal for any correction of your placement on it.

# Appointment to a Job

The eligible list of those candidates who have passed all competitive parts of the examination is in strict rank order (person with the highest mark is number 1), and eligibles are to be considered for appointments under this order. When a vacancy occurs in an agency, the three highest names on the active list are interviewed by that agency's appointing officer, and he or she can choose any of these persons. The unselected persons remain on the list, and are considered for future appointments. Number 4 on the list is certified for consideration when the next vacancy occurs. This procedure continues until the list of eligibles is exhausted or the list is declared terminated by the Department of Personnel.

## Probation

All new appointees from a civil service list are on probation usually for one year, and can be fired during that time without a stated cause. You will be informed by the agency's appointing officer if the probationary period is for a different period of time for your position.

## Investigation

For most positions, the Department of Personnel investigates the statements on your Experience Paper only after you have been appointed to a job. You will be called to the Department of Personnel, and told to bring verifications such as college transcripts, diplomas, birth certificates, etc. Your previous employers will be asked to verify that you worked for them, and that your duties were as you described them. Be sure that your Experience Paper is accurate and verifiable because you may be fired if investigation finds that you do not in fact meet the minimum requirements.

For some city positions, especially those in uniform or those responsible for handling large sums of money, investigation must be completed before appointments can be made.

If you are a physically handicapped eligible, and find placement in the right agency difficult, the Mayor's Office of the Handicapped may be able to assist you in finding the right job.

# THE REWARDS OF WORKING IN GOVERNMENT SERVICE

## Salary

The minimum salary for the job that interests you is given in the Notice of Examination. You will usually be appointed at that salary, although in some instances an agency may be willing to pay a higher salary if you have a special skill or qualification. Salary ranges for most non-managerial titles are determined after collective bargaining negotiations between the city and the union representing the majority of employees in the title. Most contracts cover a two- or three-year period, and call for wage increases during that time. You do *not* have to be a union member to receive the negotiated salary. For those titles not covered by union contracts, increases are provided to keep salaries in line with those that do receive increases by collective bargaining.

In addition, for many titles there is more than one level of assignment, and salaries increase at the higher assignments. For example, the beginning clerical title called Office Aide has three assignment levels. A competent employee may be assigned a higher level job (without taking an examination and with a higher salary) if an agency has a vacancy at that level.

## Promotion

For all competitive positions in New York City government up to and including entrance into the management level, permanent promotion in your agency is usually obtained through competitive examination open to all persons permanently employed in the lower eligible title. The Notice of Examination for any title shows the higher title(s) you may compete for once you have gained permanent appointment to the lower one. In addition, your agency can promote you to the higher title provisionally (until an exam is given for the higher title). You can obtain the title permanently only if you score well on the promotion exam, since the same strict rules for using the rank order of the list of eligibles apply.

## Job Security

Provided that you are a competent, trustworthy employee, once you have passed the probationary period you can be reasonably certain that you are secure in your job. There are strict rules governing layoffs that must be observed in the event of a fiscal crisis or if your job is to be eliminated.

## Efficiency—Merit Raises

Employees are evaluated yearly on the quality and quantity of work performed, on their cooperativeness, adherence to agency rules, and on individual initiative shown. This is a good time to iron out any problems you are having on the job, to learn what parts of your job your supervisor finds you are doing well and what parts need improvement. An agency may grant you a merit increase in pay if you are doing exceptional work, or may assign you to a higher assignment level within your title (at higher pay) if your evaluation is exceptionally good.

## Working Conditions, Benefits, Holidays

Hours of Work: The usual New York City government work week is 7 hours a day, 35 hours a week. Most jobs are 5 days a week, Monday through Friday. In some cases the nature of the work may call for a different work week (e.g., if an agency is open 7 days a week and/or around the clock, such as the Police Department or a housing project). The Notice of Examination tells you about any special hours of work connected with the job you seek. As in all endeavors, employees sometimes have to work overtime. If you must work overtime, you will either be paid for it or given compensatory time off.

## Vacation, Sick Leave, Leave With or Without Pay

1. New York City employees enjoy a most generous vacation allowance. Within limitations, sick leave and annual leave may be accrued. If you leave City service, you will be paid for accumulated unused vacation, and if you retire, for one half of your sick leave.
2. Sick leave is accumulated at the rate of 12 days a year and must be used only for personal illness.
3. New York City grants up to 4 days off with pay if a close relative dies. Other leave with pay is granted for taking promotion exams, jury duty, attendance at court under certain circumstances, and attendance as a delegate for certain union and/or veteran's activities.
4. Leave without pay is granted for confinement and for infant care (male and female employees may apply for this benefit) for up to three years after the birth.
5. If a military reservist, you may be authorized a period not to exceed 30 calendar days during a given year for military training purposes.

## Holidays

Most New York City employees covered by collective bargaining are entitled to the following holidays each year: New Year's Day, Martin Luther King's Birthday, Washington's Birthday, Lincoln's Birthday, Memorial Day, Independence Day, Labor Day, Columbus Day, Veteran's Day, Thanksgiving, Christmas, and Presidential Election Day.

After you have been appointed to a job, your agency's personnel officer will give you complete information concerning all the entitlements and working conditions noted above.

## Other Work Benefits

1. **Health Insurance:** Employees of New York City government enjoy extensive and generous health benefits including hospital care. You will have a choice of several different health benefit plans, each designed to pay all or a good portion of your medical expenses and those of your spouse and dependent children. You will pay (by your choice) the cost of extended coverage beyond the basic contract, which is taken from your pay check. The benefits continue after you retire.

   After you are hired, your agency's personnel officer will give you detailed data that will help you decide which health insurance plan best meets your needs.

2. **Workman's Compensation:** New York City functions under the Workman's Compensation Law, and you will receive appropriate compensation under its terms if you suffer injuries in the performance of an official duty.
3. **Retirement:** The City of New York provides a generous retirement plan to which both you and the city contribute.
4. **Municipal Credit Union:** As a New York City employee you may join the Municipal Credit Union, a multi-service bank that gives generous interest on accounts, checking privileges, low-cost loans, and fills other banking needs.

## The Unions and City Employment

1. Although New York City government employees are not allowed by law to strike, a large percentage of titles in the city government are represented by unions whose primary function is to collectively bargain on salary matters. You do not have to belong to the union, but if a union has the right to bargain for your title, you will be assessed the amount of union dues, and will in any case be entitled to many union benefits.
2. In addition to bargaining on salary, the unions bargain for employee welfare benefits paid for by the city. Each union uses its funds differently. Benefits presently included by various unions are the following: supple-

mentary health benefits, including hearing aid plans; podiatry services; dental benefits; vision care benefits; scholarships; legal aid services; survivor's health benefits; and drug plans and life insurance plans. Some of these are free for you and even for your family; others provide benefits at relatively low cost.

3. The unions also provide educational services and training courses to take promotion exams. They will also assist you in grievance and disciplinary matters, if you should require it.

4. Once you are employed in a title covered by collective bargaining, a union representative will give you complete details about the union and its functions.

## Other Points You Should Know

1. **Suggestion Program:** The New York City government encourages all employees to suggest improved methods of performing not only their jobs, but any function performed in the city. Recognition, including cash awards, is possible for an employee whose suggestion or innovation is accepted and results in savings or improved service.

2. **Disciplinary Procedures:** After you have been hired by an agency, you will be told about the standards of conduct expected of all employees, the grounds for which disciplinary actions may be taken, and the procedures involved, including your right to assistance from union staff and/or legal counsel, appeals procedures, and the penalties for infractions of agency and City/State rules.

# GLOSSARY OF PERSONNEL TERMS USED IN NEW YORK CITY

## 1. Classification Terminology

**Career Ladder**—Another expression for the series of successively higher titles to which a competitive employee can move through promotion exams—from entrance levels to administrative (managerial) levels.

**Class of Positions**—All positions that are sufficiently similar in the scope of their duties and responsibilities to require the same qualification requirements, tests, and salary range.

**Class Specification**—Formal description of a class of positions indicating factors common to all the positions, showing the kind of work being done, level of difficulty and responsibility, degree of supervision received and exercised over others, minimum requirements needed to fill the position, and the line of promotion to this class of positions and also to the next higher one.

**Competitive Class**—Positions for which it is practical to test competitively for merit and fitness.

**Exempt Class**—Positions which encompass duties for which neither competitive nor non-competitive examinations are practical, e.g., confidentiality positions.

**Labor Relations Order/Personnel Order/Implementing Personnel Order**—Various types of orders reflecting establishment of new titles, original salary ranges, and later salary changes for titles.

**Management Pay Plan**—The pay plan for management level positions. It is composed of a number of assignment levels reflecting progressively higher levels of responsibility and higher pay. Movement from one assignment level to another is possible without passing an examination.

**Management Position**—These are the highest levels of competitive class positions in an occupation, and are generally concerned with administering/managing/supervising and/or doing highly professional/technical work. Entrance to these positions can be by promotion examination. If there are insufficient eligibles in the lower title in the occupation involved, a competitive examination among anyone meeting the qualification requirements may also be held. (This latter exam is called an open-competitive examination.) Persons on the promotion list must be considered for appointment before the list from the open-competitive list can be used.

**Non-competitive Class**—Positions for which competitive examination is not practical, a non-competitive exam is given, e.g., nurse.

**Occupational Group**—Classification of one or more series of titles into a larger group all having a degree of similarity in duties. That is, separate series of typist titles, clerk titles, office appliance operators, and bookkeeper titles might be classified into one occupational group called the Clerical Occupational Group.

**Original Jurisdiction**—Salary determination made by the City Personnel Director and the Director of the Office of Management and Budget for classes of positions that are not represented by unions in collective bargaining negotiations for salary increases.

**Position**—A specific job to be performed by an individual consisting of all the current major duties and responsibilities assigned or delegated by management.

**Position Allocation**—The process by which the duties and responsibilities of an individual (i.e., a position) is placed (allocated) into a class of positions.

**Position Classification**—Analyzing and categorizing jobs by occupational group, series, class, and grade according to like duties, responsibilities, and qualification requirements.

**Series**—Several classes of positions that are in the same occupational field, but have progressively more responsible duties, less supervision, and have increasing supervisory responsibility (e.g., Buyer, Senior Buyer, Supervising Buyer). Permanent appointment to a higher title is by competitive promotion from the lower title.

**Title**—Identification of a class of positions, e.g., Office Aide.

## 2. Examinations Terminology

**Accredited Institution**—College or institution of higher education, which, after study of the quality of the teaching staff, nature of the curriculum, and other factors has been found "accredited" by certain state, regional, or national accrediting bodies. Note: The Notice of Examination for titles for which a college degree is required usually specify that such a degree must be from an accredited college or university.

**Affirmative Action**—A policy that requires agencies to take positive steps to ensure equal opportunity in employment, development, advancement, and treatment of all employees and applications for employment regardless of race, sex, religion, age, national origin, or physical or mental handicap. Affirmative Action also requires that specific actions be directed at the special problems and unique concerns in assuring equal employment opportunity for minorities and women.

**Agency**—Any City department, administration board, commission, or authority that uses competitive examinations prepared by or under the supervision of the New York City Department of Personnel. This includes non-pedagogical titles in the Board of Education, and positions in the Housing Authority and Transit Authority.

**Appeals**—Disagreement by a candidate of his or her assigned rating on examinations.

**Application Form**—The formal application blank which every candidate must complete.

**Certification List**—A list of eligibles ranked, according to regulations, for consideration for an appointment or a promotion.

**Competitive Test(s)**—The Test(s) that rank candidates in order of their ratings. The combined ratings of all the competitive tests (taking into consideration their respective weights) will result in a rank order list of eligibles, and appointments made in rank order in accordance with established rules and regulations.

In an examination, one or more of the following types of tests are given:

1. Multiple Choice Test (objective).
2. Written Test—Such as essay or short answer test (subjective).
3. Oral Test—Can be an individual oral exam testing technical knowledge, group problem solving oral testing communication skill, or several other types of tests.
4. Physical Test—Competitively rating your ability to do the required physical activities of the job, e.g., lifting, running, etc.
5. Practical—Competitively testing your ability to do the required work or job. For example, a practical test for a dentist might competitively evaluate ability to make and fit dentures.
6. Education and Experience Test—An unassembled test wherein education, training, and experience are rated competitively.

**Entrance Level Position**—A position in an occupational group at the beginning level or grade.

**Equal Employment Opportunity (EEO Guidelines)**—Federal guidelines used by the New York City Department of Personnel to ensure that the entire examination procedure is free from any discrimination as to race, sex, religion, national origin, or mental or physical handicap; that the exam is related to the duties required by incumbents of the positions being examined for; and fairly tests the knowledge, skills, and abilities needed to successfully perform that job.

**Examination**—A means of measuring, in a practical and suitable manner, relative qualifications of applicants for employment in specific positions.

**Examination Procedure**—All the steps you need to take to obtain permanent employment with New York City government. They include filing, meeting minimum requirements, taking and passing all tests (including competitive and qualifying tests), appointment to the job being investigated, and successfully completing the probationary period. (Also called the Selection Process.)

**Experience Paper—Form A**—An official part of a New York City Civil Service exam in which a candidate indicates his or her qualifications to take the competitive examination. If there is no test other than an evaluation of education and experience, the Experience Paper becomes a major part of the actual exam, and the data given is competitively rated.

**Form DP 398 (Foreign Education Evaluation)**—Application to request the Department of Personnel to evaluate a candidate's foreign education to determine comparability with education received in accredited educational institutions in the U.S.

**General Examination Regulations/General Provisions of the Notice of Examination**—Official Documents giving regulations pertinent to the examination procedure. They are considered to be part of the Notice of Examination, and all candidates are expected to be familiar with their contents. They are posted and copies are available in the Applications Division of the Department of Personnel.

**Key Answers**—Final correct answers to multiple-choice questions published by the Department of Personnel.

**Notice of Examination**—The most important document to read and understand. It tells everything you need to know about the job, including duties, entrance salary, minimum requirements, test, promotion opportunity, etc.

**Permanent Appointment**—Status of an individual after both successful competition with others for the same position and successful completion of the probationary period.

**Pool**—A method by which a number of eligibles for a specific title are interviewed, in one session and at one location, by personnel officers from several agencies for vacant positions in their agencies.

**Preference, Veteran**—The statutory right to special advantages in appointment or separations, based on a person's discharge under conditions acceptable to the Department of Personnel after active duty in the military service during specified periods.

**Probationary Period**—A trail period that is a condition of the initial competitive appointment, and of subsequent promotions. This provides the final indispensable test of ability—that of actual performance of the job. A person on probation can be dismissed during that period without a reason being given.

**Promotion, Competitive**—Selection of a permanent civil service employee for a higher position, using procedures that evaluates candidates based on merit and fitness.

**Provisional Appointment**—Non-permanent appointment to a competitive class position until a list of eligibles is established after a competitive test and a permanent appointment is made. Persons appointed provisionally must meet the qualification requirements listed in the class specification for their position.

**Qualifying Test**—A test given to those candidates who have passed the competitive test, and must also prove that they can do such tasks as the following:

1. Successfully do certain physical activities required on the job (e.g., lift 50 pound bags)
2. Speak and understand a foreign language
3. Are medically qualified to perform the duties of the job
4. By passing a written test, that they have certain basic knowledge of how to handle the job requirements, and/or can read and write English.

Read the Notice of Examination carefully to understand the nature of the competitive and qualifying tests you must take to obtain a permanent job in the field you have chosen.

**Requirements** (Also called **Mimimum Requirements** or **Qualifications Requirements)**—The minimum experience and/or education which a candidate must possess in order to be competitively rated in an examination.

**Selective Certification**—In connection with jobs for which competitive written exams are given, some assignments within a title may have to be filled by persons who, in addition to having passed the competitive exam, must also be proficient in certain specific skills which were not tested (e.g., a skill such as speaking a language other than English).

**Tests**—The method by which and the degree to which the specific knowledge, skills, and abilities needed to perform a particular job are examined and rated for each job. Tests can be *assembled* tests where many candidates are called together and tested at one time; or an *unassembled* test, which is most frequently a competitive test of your education, training, and experience with no gathering of fellow candidates.

**Weighted Tests**—An examination may consist of two or more tests. The relative importance of the two are weighted on the basis of 100%. If the examination consists, for example, of a multiple choice test and an essay test, the multiple choice one may be weighted 60% and the essay weighted 40%. Your marks on each test are accordingly weighted 60% and 40% respectively in arriving at your rating for the entire examination.

## 3. Other Personnel Terminology

**Collective Bargaining**—Negotiations between the City and a union having been certified as representing the employees in a particular title on matters deemed "bargainable," including salaries, welfare funds, working conditions, etc.

**Grievance**—A complaint by an employee or group of employees about alleged infractions of either Department of Personnel, agency, or New York State rules or regulations, or of a provision of a collective bargaining agreement, or about an aspect of the working conditions that concerns them.

**Leave, Annual**—Time allowed to employees for vacation and personal business.

**Personnel Action**—The process necessary to appoint, separate, reinstate, or make other changes affecting an employee (e.g., change in position, assignment, tenure, etc.).

**Retirement Allowance**—The amount of money you will receive when you retire, i.e., your pension.

**Union Shop**—New York City government labor relations term for the situation when all persons in a title for which a union has been certified as the bargaining union are required to pay dues to the union, and if they choose not to join, they are to be extended the same privileges and benefits as those who do.

| SOCIAL SECURITY NO. | DEPARTMENT OF PERSONNEL<br>49 Thomas Street, New York, N.Y. 10013<br>**EXPERIENCE PAPER** | FORM A<br>EXAMINATION NO. |
|---|---|---|
| ___/___/___ | Exact Title of Examination | |

**DO NOT WRITE IN THIS SPACE**

| Not qualified under terms of advertisement | QUALIFIED: Admitted for further examination pending final determination of qualifications. | RATING |
|---|---|---|
| | | |

**To Investigator:** Verify items checked and also data mentioned here ..............................

☐ If this box is checked, submit a report with full details to ..............................

**FOLLOW THESE INSTRUCTIONS CAREFULLY:**

a. Type, print or write (in blue or black ink) the information requested.
b. Be COMPLETE, CONCISE AND ACCURATE. The information you enter below will be used to determine your rating on training and experience. If statements of material facts are found to be false, exaggerated or misleading, you may be disqualified.
c. DO NOT REVEAL YOUR IDENTITY in any way on this experience paper. If you are or have been in business for yourself or have been employed by a relative of the same name, write "self" or the relationship of the relative in the space headed "Name of Employer".

**1. LICENSE OR REGISTRATION:** If a license or registration is required, answer the following.

a. Title of lic. or reg. you possess which is valid in New York City .................... License or Registration No. ....................
b. Name of issuing agency ....................
c. Date of original issue .................... Date last renewed or registered .................... Renewal number .................... Date of expiration ....................

**2. EDUCATION:** **3. DATE OF BIRTH*** ....................

| Give Name and Locations of Schools Below | Day or Night | From Mo. | From Yr. | To Mo. | To Yr. | Were you Graduated (Yes or No) | Degree Received | Total Credits Completed | Major Subject | No. of Credits in Major |
|---|---|---|---|---|---|---|---|---|---|---|
| High School or Trade School | | | | | | | | | | |
| | | | | | | | | | | |
| College or other School | | | | | | | | | | |
| | | | | | | | | | | |

**4. List below any courses which you have passed which: (a) are necessary to meet the minimum requirements for the position; (b) provide training appropriate to the position; (c) are in related fields.**

| NAME OF COLLEGE OR INSTITUTION | Course Number | EXACT TITLE OF COURSE (Place "G" after graduate courses) | No. of Credits | Date Completed |
|---|---|---|---|---|
| | | | | |
| | | | | |
| | | | | |
| | | | | |
| | | | | |
| | | | | |
| | | | | |

*The New York Human Rights Law prohibits discrimination on the basis of age, creed, color, national origin, sex, disability or marital status of any individual. The law allows certain age or sex specifications if based upon a bona fide occupational qualification or statutory authorization.

**QUALIFYING EMPLOYMENT.** List in chronological order those positions you have held which tend to qualify you for the position sought. Begin with the present or most recent position. Use a separate block for each position. List as a separate employment every material change of duties although with the same employer. Include pertinent experience or training in the armed forces.

**1**

| Dates of Employment (give month and year) From To | Length of Employment Yrs. Mos. | Exact Title of Your Position | Starting Salary per Last Salary per |
|---|---|---|---|
| Name and Address of Employer | | Nature of Employer's Business | |
| Number and Titles of Employees You Supervise | | Title (not name) of your Immediate Superior | |
| | | If with New York City or State was this a provisional appointment? Yes ☐ No ☐ | No. of Hours Worked per Week |
| Describe Your Duties | | | |

**2**

| Dates of Employment (give month and year) From To | Length of Employment Yrs. Mos. | Exact Title of Your Position | Starting Salary per Last Salary per |
|---|---|---|---|
| Name and Address of Employer | | Nature of Employer's Business | |
| Number and Titles of Employees You Supervise | | Title (not name) of your Immediate Superior | |
| | | If with New York City or State was this a provisional appointment? Yes ☐ No ☐ | No. of Hours Worked per Week |
| Describe Your Duties | | | |

**3**

| Dates of Employment (give month and year) From To | Length of Employment Yrs. Mos. | Exact Title of Your Position | Starting Salary per Last Salary per |
|---|---|---|---|
| Name and Address of Employer | | Nature of Employer's Business | |
| Number and Titles of Employees You Supervise | | Title (not name) of your Immediate Superior | |
| | | If with New York City or State was this a provisional appointment? Yes ☐ No ☐ | No. of Hours Worked per Week |
| Describe Your Duties | | | |

**4**

| Dates of Employment (give month and year) From To | Length of Employment Yrs. Mos. | Exact Title of Your Position | Starting Salary per Last Salary per |
|---|---|---|---|
| Name and Address of Employer | | Nature of Employer's Business | |
| Number and Titles of Employees You Supervise | | Title (not name) of your Immediate Superior | |
| | | If with New York City or State was this a provisional appointment? Yes ☐ No ☐ | No. of Hours Worked per Week |
| Describe Your Duties | | | |

| OTHER EXPERIENCE: List here only the other employments you have had which were not included before. | | | | | |
|---|---|---|---|---|---|
| Dates of Employment | | Name and Address of Employer | Business of Employer | Title of Your Position and Highest Salary | Brief Description of Duties You Performed |
| From | To | | | | |
| | | | | | |
| | | | | | |
| | | | | | |
| | | | | | |
| | | | | | |
| | | | | | |

Any additional qualifications you have for the position may be listed here; for example: field work in connection with training, authorship or co-authorship of books or of articles in recognized journals, special certification from professional boards, other professional attainments, etc. (Caution: Do not mention your name.) Additional courses or experience may also be listed here.

**IF YOU HAVE ADDITIONAL QUALIFYING EXPERIENCE, ATTACH SEPARATE PAPER USING THE SAME FORMAT**

# Part Two

# *Sample Examinations for Practice*

# SAMPLE ANSWER SHEET
# FOR SAMPLE PRACTICE EXAMINATION I

| | | | | |
|---|---|---|---|---|
| 1 Ⓐ Ⓑ Ⓒ Ⓓ | 17 Ⓐ Ⓑ Ⓒ Ⓓ | 33 Ⓐ Ⓑ Ⓒ Ⓓ | 49 Ⓐ Ⓑ Ⓒ Ⓓ | 65 Ⓐ Ⓑ Ⓒ Ⓓ |
| 2 Ⓐ Ⓑ Ⓒ Ⓓ | 18 Ⓐ Ⓑ Ⓒ Ⓓ | 34 Ⓐ Ⓑ Ⓒ Ⓓ | 50 Ⓐ Ⓑ Ⓒ Ⓓ | 66 Ⓐ Ⓑ Ⓒ Ⓓ |
| 3 Ⓐ Ⓑ Ⓒ Ⓓ | 19 Ⓐ Ⓑ Ⓒ Ⓓ | 35 Ⓐ Ⓑ Ⓒ Ⓓ | 51 Ⓐ Ⓑ Ⓒ Ⓓ | 67 Ⓐ Ⓑ Ⓒ Ⓓ |
| 4 Ⓐ Ⓑ Ⓒ Ⓓ | 20 Ⓐ Ⓑ Ⓒ Ⓓ | 36 Ⓐ Ⓑ Ⓒ Ⓓ | 52 Ⓐ Ⓑ Ⓒ Ⓓ | 68 Ⓐ Ⓑ Ⓒ Ⓓ |
| 5 Ⓐ Ⓑ Ⓒ Ⓓ | 21 Ⓐ Ⓑ Ⓒ Ⓓ | 37 Ⓐ Ⓑ Ⓒ Ⓓ | 53 Ⓐ Ⓑ Ⓒ Ⓓ | 69 Ⓐ Ⓑ Ⓒ Ⓓ |
| 6 Ⓐ Ⓑ Ⓒ Ⓓ | 22 Ⓐ Ⓑ Ⓒ Ⓓ | 38 Ⓐ Ⓑ Ⓒ Ⓓ | 54 Ⓐ Ⓑ Ⓒ Ⓓ | 70 Ⓐ Ⓑ Ⓒ Ⓓ |
| 7 Ⓐ Ⓑ Ⓒ Ⓓ | 23 Ⓐ Ⓑ Ⓒ Ⓓ | 39 Ⓐ Ⓑ Ⓒ Ⓓ | 55 Ⓐ Ⓑ Ⓒ Ⓓ | 71 Ⓐ Ⓑ Ⓒ Ⓓ |
| 8 Ⓐ Ⓑ Ⓒ Ⓓ | 24 Ⓐ Ⓑ Ⓒ Ⓓ | 40 Ⓐ Ⓑ Ⓒ Ⓓ | 56 Ⓐ Ⓑ Ⓒ Ⓓ | 72 Ⓐ Ⓑ Ⓒ Ⓓ |
| 9 Ⓐ Ⓑ Ⓒ Ⓓ | 25 Ⓐ Ⓑ Ⓒ Ⓓ | 41 Ⓐ Ⓑ Ⓒ Ⓓ | 57 Ⓐ Ⓑ Ⓒ Ⓓ | 73 Ⓐ Ⓑ Ⓒ Ⓓ |
| 10 Ⓐ Ⓑ Ⓒ Ⓓ | 26 Ⓐ Ⓑ Ⓒ Ⓓ | 42 Ⓐ Ⓑ Ⓒ Ⓓ | 58 Ⓐ Ⓑ Ⓒ Ⓓ | 74 Ⓐ Ⓑ Ⓒ Ⓓ |
| 11 Ⓐ Ⓑ Ⓒ Ⓓ | 27 Ⓐ Ⓑ Ⓒ Ⓓ | 43 Ⓐ Ⓑ Ⓒ Ⓓ | 59 Ⓐ Ⓑ Ⓒ Ⓓ | 75 Ⓐ Ⓑ Ⓒ Ⓓ |
| 12 Ⓐ Ⓑ Ⓒ Ⓓ | 28 Ⓐ Ⓑ Ⓒ Ⓓ | 44 Ⓐ Ⓑ Ⓒ Ⓓ | 60 Ⓐ Ⓑ Ⓒ Ⓓ | 76 Ⓐ Ⓑ Ⓒ Ⓓ |
| 13 Ⓐ Ⓑ Ⓒ Ⓓ | 29 Ⓐ Ⓑ Ⓒ Ⓓ | 45 Ⓐ Ⓑ Ⓒ Ⓓ | 61 Ⓐ Ⓑ Ⓒ Ⓓ | 77 Ⓐ Ⓑ Ⓒ Ⓓ |
| 14 Ⓐ Ⓑ Ⓒ Ⓓ | 30 Ⓐ Ⓑ Ⓒ Ⓓ | 46 Ⓐ Ⓑ Ⓒ Ⓓ | 62 Ⓐ Ⓑ Ⓒ Ⓓ | 78 Ⓐ Ⓑ Ⓒ Ⓓ |
| 15 Ⓐ Ⓑ Ⓒ Ⓓ | 31 Ⓐ Ⓑ Ⓒ Ⓓ | 47 Ⓐ Ⓑ Ⓒ Ⓓ | 63 Ⓐ Ⓑ Ⓒ Ⓓ | 79 Ⓐ Ⓑ Ⓒ Ⓓ |
| 16 Ⓐ Ⓑ Ⓒ Ⓓ | 32 Ⓐ Ⓑ Ⓒ Ⓓ | 48 Ⓐ Ⓑ Ⓒ Ⓓ | 64 Ⓐ Ⓑ Ⓒ Ⓓ | 80 Ⓐ Ⓑ Ⓒ Ⓓ |

# SAMPLE ANSWER SHEET
# FOR SAMPLE PRACTICE EXAMINATION II

| | | | | |
|---|---|---|---|---|
| 1 Ⓐ Ⓑ Ⓒ Ⓓ | 17 Ⓐ Ⓑ Ⓒ | 33 Ⓐ Ⓑ Ⓒ Ⓓ Ⓔ | 49 Ⓐ Ⓑ Ⓒ | 65 Ⓐ Ⓑ Ⓒ Ⓓ |
| 2 Ⓐ Ⓑ | 18 Ⓐ Ⓑ Ⓒ Ⓓ | 34 Ⓐ Ⓑ Ⓒ | 50 Ⓐ Ⓑ Ⓒ | 66 Ⓐ Ⓑ Ⓒ Ⓓ |
| 3 Ⓐ Ⓑ | 19 Ⓐ Ⓑ Ⓒ Ⓓ | 35 Ⓐ Ⓑ Ⓒ | 51 Ⓐ Ⓑ Ⓒ | 67 Ⓐ Ⓑ Ⓒ Ⓓ |
| 4 Ⓐ Ⓑ | 20 Ⓐ Ⓑ Ⓒ Ⓓ | 36 Ⓐ Ⓑ Ⓒ | 52 Ⓐ Ⓑ Ⓒ Ⓓ | 68 Ⓐ Ⓑ Ⓒ Ⓓ |
| 5 Ⓐ Ⓑ | 21 Ⓐ Ⓑ Ⓒ Ⓓ | 37 Ⓐ Ⓑ Ⓒ | 53 Ⓐ Ⓑ Ⓒ Ⓓ | 69 Ⓐ Ⓑ Ⓒ Ⓓ |
| 6 Ⓐ Ⓑ | 22 Ⓐ Ⓑ Ⓒ Ⓓ | 38 Ⓐ Ⓑ Ⓒ Ⓓ | 54 Ⓐ Ⓑ Ⓒ Ⓓ | 70 Ⓐ Ⓑ Ⓒ Ⓓ |
| 7 Ⓐ Ⓑ Ⓒ Ⓓ | 23 Ⓐ Ⓑ | 39 Ⓐ Ⓑ Ⓒ Ⓓ | 55 Ⓐ Ⓑ Ⓒ Ⓓ | 71 Ⓐ Ⓑ Ⓒ Ⓓ |
| 8 Ⓐ Ⓑ Ⓒ Ⓓ | 24 Ⓐ Ⓑ | 40 Ⓐ Ⓑ Ⓒ Ⓓ | 56 Ⓐ Ⓑ Ⓒ Ⓓ | 72 Ⓐ Ⓑ Ⓒ Ⓓ |
| 9 Ⓐ Ⓑ Ⓒ | 25 Ⓐ Ⓑ | 41 Ⓐ Ⓑ Ⓒ Ⓓ | 57 Ⓐ Ⓑ Ⓒ Ⓓ | 73 Ⓐ Ⓑ Ⓒ Ⓓ |
| 10 Ⓐ Ⓑ Ⓒ | 26 Ⓐ Ⓑ | 42 Ⓐ Ⓑ Ⓒ Ⓓ | 58 Ⓐ Ⓑ Ⓒ Ⓓ | 74 Ⓐ Ⓑ Ⓒ Ⓓ |
| 11 Ⓐ Ⓑ Ⓒ | 27 Ⓐ Ⓑ Ⓒ Ⓓ | 43 Ⓐ Ⓑ Ⓒ Ⓓ | 59 Ⓐ Ⓑ Ⓒ Ⓓ | 75 Ⓐ Ⓑ Ⓒ Ⓓ |
| 12 Ⓐ Ⓑ Ⓒ | 28 Ⓐ Ⓑ Ⓒ Ⓓ | 44 Ⓐ Ⓑ Ⓒ | 60 Ⓐ Ⓑ Ⓒ Ⓓ | 76 Ⓐ Ⓑ Ⓒ Ⓓ |
| 13 Ⓐ Ⓑ Ⓒ | 29 Ⓐ Ⓑ Ⓒ Ⓓ Ⓔ | 45 Ⓐ Ⓑ Ⓒ | 61 Ⓐ Ⓑ Ⓒ Ⓓ | 77 Ⓐ Ⓑ Ⓒ Ⓓ |
| 14 Ⓐ Ⓑ Ⓒ | 30 Ⓐ Ⓑ Ⓒ Ⓓ Ⓔ | 46 Ⓐ Ⓑ Ⓒ | 62 Ⓐ Ⓑ Ⓒ Ⓓ | 78 Ⓐ Ⓑ Ⓒ Ⓓ |
| 15 Ⓐ Ⓑ Ⓒ | 31 Ⓐ Ⓑ Ⓒ Ⓓ Ⓔ | 47 Ⓐ Ⓑ Ⓒ | 63 Ⓐ Ⓑ Ⓒ Ⓓ | 79 Ⓐ Ⓑ Ⓒ Ⓓ |
| 16 Ⓐ Ⓑ Ⓒ | 32 Ⓐ Ⓑ Ⓒ Ⓓ Ⓔ | 48 Ⓐ Ⓑ Ⓒ | 64 Ⓐ Ⓑ Ⓒ Ⓓ | 80 Ⓐ Ⓑ Ⓒ Ⓓ |

# SAMPLE ANSWER SHEET
# FOR SAMPLE PRACTICE EXAMINATION III

| | | | | |
|---|---|---|---|---|
| 1 Ⓐ Ⓑ Ⓒ Ⓓ | 21 Ⓐ Ⓑ Ⓒ Ⓓ | 41 Ⓐ Ⓑ Ⓒ | 61 Ⓐ Ⓑ Ⓒ Ⓓ | 81 Ⓐ Ⓑ Ⓒ Ⓓ |
| 2 Ⓐ Ⓑ Ⓒ Ⓓ | 22 Ⓐ Ⓑ Ⓒ Ⓓ | 42 Ⓐ Ⓑ Ⓒ | 62 Ⓐ Ⓑ Ⓒ | 82 Ⓐ Ⓑ Ⓒ Ⓓ |
| 3 Ⓐ Ⓑ Ⓒ Ⓓ | 23 Ⓐ Ⓑ Ⓒ Ⓓ | 43 Ⓐ Ⓑ Ⓒ | 63 Ⓐ Ⓑ Ⓒ | 83 Ⓐ Ⓑ Ⓒ Ⓓ |
| 4 Ⓐ Ⓑ Ⓒ Ⓓ | 24 Ⓐ Ⓑ Ⓒ Ⓓ | 44 Ⓐ Ⓑ Ⓒ | 64 Ⓐ Ⓑ Ⓒ | 84 Ⓐ Ⓑ Ⓒ Ⓓ |
| 5 Ⓐ Ⓑ Ⓒ Ⓓ | 25 Ⓐ Ⓑ Ⓒ Ⓓ | 45 Ⓐ Ⓑ Ⓒ | 65 Ⓐ Ⓑ Ⓒ | 85 Ⓐ Ⓑ Ⓒ Ⓓ |
| 6 Ⓐ Ⓑ Ⓒ Ⓓ | 26 Ⓐ Ⓑ Ⓒ Ⓓ Ⓔ | 46 Ⓐ Ⓑ Ⓒ Ⓓ | 66 Ⓐ Ⓑ Ⓒ Ⓓ | 86 Ⓐ Ⓑ Ⓒ Ⓓ |
| 7 Ⓐ Ⓑ Ⓒ Ⓓ | 27 Ⓐ Ⓑ Ⓒ Ⓓ Ⓔ | 47 Ⓐ Ⓑ Ⓒ Ⓓ | 67 Ⓐ Ⓑ Ⓒ Ⓓ | 87 Ⓐ Ⓑ Ⓒ Ⓓ |
| 8 Ⓐ Ⓑ Ⓒ Ⓓ | 28 Ⓐ Ⓑ Ⓒ Ⓓ Ⓔ | 48 Ⓐ Ⓑ Ⓒ Ⓓ | 68 Ⓐ Ⓑ Ⓒ Ⓓ | 88 Ⓐ Ⓑ Ⓒ Ⓓ |
| 9 Ⓐ Ⓑ Ⓒ Ⓓ | 29 Ⓐ Ⓑ Ⓒ Ⓓ Ⓔ | 49 Ⓐ Ⓑ Ⓒ Ⓓ | 69 Ⓐ Ⓑ Ⓒ Ⓓ | 89 Ⓐ Ⓑ Ⓒ Ⓓ |
| 10 Ⓐ Ⓑ Ⓒ Ⓓ | 30 Ⓐ Ⓑ Ⓒ Ⓓ Ⓔ | 50 Ⓐ Ⓑ Ⓒ Ⓓ | 70 Ⓐ Ⓑ Ⓒ Ⓓ | 90 Ⓐ Ⓑ Ⓒ Ⓓ |
| 11 Ⓐ Ⓑ Ⓒ Ⓓ | 31 Ⓐ Ⓑ Ⓒ Ⓓ | 51 Ⓐ Ⓑ Ⓒ Ⓓ | 71 Ⓐ Ⓑ Ⓒ Ⓓ | 91 Ⓐ Ⓑ Ⓒ Ⓓ |
| 12 Ⓐ Ⓑ Ⓒ Ⓓ | 32 Ⓐ Ⓑ Ⓒ Ⓓ | 52 Ⓐ Ⓑ Ⓒ Ⓓ | 72 Ⓐ Ⓑ Ⓒ Ⓓ | 92 Ⓐ Ⓑ Ⓒ Ⓓ |
| 13 Ⓐ Ⓑ Ⓒ Ⓓ | 33 Ⓐ Ⓑ Ⓒ Ⓓ | 53 Ⓐ Ⓑ Ⓒ Ⓓ | 73 Ⓐ Ⓑ Ⓒ Ⓓ | 93 Ⓐ Ⓑ Ⓒ Ⓓ |
| 14 Ⓐ Ⓑ Ⓒ Ⓓ | 34 Ⓐ Ⓑ Ⓒ Ⓓ | 54 Ⓐ Ⓑ Ⓒ Ⓓ | 74 Ⓐ Ⓑ Ⓒ Ⓓ | 94 Ⓐ Ⓑ Ⓒ Ⓓ |
| 15 Ⓐ Ⓑ Ⓒ Ⓓ | 35 Ⓐ Ⓑ Ⓒ Ⓓ | 55 Ⓐ Ⓑ Ⓒ Ⓓ | 75 Ⓐ Ⓑ | 95 Ⓐ Ⓑ Ⓒ Ⓓ |
| 16 Ⓐ Ⓑ Ⓒ Ⓓ | 36 Ⓐ Ⓑ Ⓒ Ⓓ | 56 Ⓐ Ⓑ Ⓒ Ⓓ | 76 Ⓐ Ⓑ | 96 Ⓐ Ⓑ Ⓒ Ⓓ |
| 17 Ⓐ Ⓑ Ⓒ Ⓓ | 37 Ⓐ Ⓑ Ⓒ Ⓓ | 57 Ⓐ Ⓑ Ⓒ Ⓓ | 77 Ⓐ Ⓑ | 97 Ⓐ Ⓑ Ⓒ Ⓓ |
| 18 Ⓐ Ⓑ Ⓒ Ⓓ | 38 Ⓐ Ⓑ Ⓒ Ⓓ | 58 Ⓐ Ⓑ Ⓒ Ⓓ | 78 Ⓐ Ⓑ | 98 Ⓐ Ⓑ Ⓒ Ⓓ |
| 19 Ⓐ Ⓑ Ⓒ Ⓓ | 39 Ⓐ Ⓑ Ⓒ Ⓓ | 59 Ⓐ Ⓑ Ⓒ Ⓓ | 79 Ⓐ Ⓑ | 99 Ⓐ Ⓑ Ⓒ Ⓓ |
| 20 Ⓐ Ⓑ Ⓒ Ⓓ | 40 Ⓐ Ⓑ Ⓒ Ⓓ | 60 Ⓐ Ⓑ Ⓒ Ⓓ | 80 Ⓐ Ⓑ | 100 Ⓐ Ⓑ Ⓒ Ⓓ |

# SAMPLE ANSWER SHEET
# FOR SAMPLE PRACTICE EXAMINATION IV

| | | | | |
|---|---|---|---|---|
| 1 Ⓐ Ⓑ Ⓒ Ⓓ | 19 Ⓐ Ⓑ Ⓒ Ⓓ | 37 Ⓐ Ⓑ Ⓒ Ⓓ | 55 Ⓐ Ⓑ Ⓒ Ⓓ | 73 Ⓐ Ⓑ Ⓒ Ⓓ |
| 2 Ⓐ Ⓑ Ⓒ Ⓓ | 20 Ⓐ Ⓑ Ⓒ Ⓓ | 38 Ⓐ Ⓑ Ⓒ Ⓓ | 56 Ⓐ Ⓑ Ⓒ Ⓓ | 74 Ⓐ Ⓑ Ⓒ Ⓓ |
| 3 Ⓐ Ⓑ Ⓒ Ⓓ | 21 Ⓐ Ⓑ Ⓒ Ⓓ | 39 Ⓐ Ⓑ Ⓒ Ⓓ | 57 Ⓐ Ⓑ Ⓒ Ⓓ | 75 Ⓐ Ⓑ Ⓒ Ⓓ |
| 4 Ⓐ Ⓑ Ⓒ Ⓓ | 22 Ⓐ Ⓑ Ⓒ Ⓓ | 40 Ⓐ Ⓑ Ⓒ Ⓓ | 58 Ⓐ Ⓑ Ⓒ Ⓓ | 76 Ⓐ Ⓑ Ⓒ Ⓓ |
| 5 Ⓐ Ⓑ Ⓒ Ⓓ | 23 Ⓐ Ⓑ Ⓒ Ⓓ | 41 Ⓐ Ⓑ | 59 Ⓐ Ⓑ Ⓒ Ⓓ | 77 Ⓐ Ⓑ Ⓒ Ⓓ |
| 6 Ⓐ Ⓑ Ⓒ Ⓓ | 24 Ⓐ Ⓑ Ⓒ Ⓓ | 42 Ⓐ Ⓑ | 60 Ⓐ Ⓑ Ⓒ Ⓓ | 78 Ⓐ Ⓑ Ⓒ Ⓓ |
| 7 Ⓐ Ⓑ Ⓒ Ⓓ | 25 Ⓐ Ⓑ Ⓒ Ⓓ | 43 Ⓐ Ⓑ | 61 Ⓐ Ⓑ Ⓒ Ⓓ | 79 Ⓐ Ⓑ Ⓒ Ⓓ |
| 8 Ⓐ Ⓑ Ⓒ Ⓓ | 26 Ⓐ Ⓑ Ⓒ Ⓓ | 44 Ⓐ Ⓑ | 62 Ⓐ Ⓑ Ⓒ Ⓓ | 80 Ⓐ Ⓑ Ⓒ Ⓓ |
| 9 Ⓐ Ⓑ Ⓒ Ⓓ | 27 Ⓐ Ⓑ Ⓒ Ⓓ | 45 Ⓐ Ⓑ | 63 Ⓐ Ⓑ Ⓒ Ⓓ | 81 Ⓐ Ⓑ Ⓒ Ⓓ |
| 10 Ⓐ Ⓑ Ⓒ Ⓓ | 28 Ⓐ Ⓑ Ⓒ Ⓓ | 46 Ⓐ Ⓑ | 64 Ⓐ Ⓑ Ⓒ Ⓓ | 82 Ⓐ Ⓑ Ⓒ Ⓓ |
| 11 Ⓐ Ⓑ Ⓒ Ⓓ | 29 Ⓐ Ⓑ Ⓒ Ⓓ | 47 Ⓐ Ⓑ Ⓒ Ⓓ | 65 Ⓐ Ⓑ Ⓒ Ⓓ | 83 Ⓐ Ⓑ Ⓒ Ⓓ |
| 12 Ⓐ Ⓑ Ⓒ Ⓓ | 30 Ⓐ Ⓑ Ⓒ Ⓓ | 48 Ⓐ Ⓑ Ⓒ Ⓓ | 66 Ⓐ Ⓑ Ⓒ Ⓓ | 84 Ⓐ Ⓑ Ⓒ Ⓓ |
| 13 Ⓐ Ⓑ Ⓒ Ⓓ | 31 Ⓐ Ⓑ Ⓒ Ⓓ | 49 Ⓐ Ⓑ Ⓒ Ⓓ | 67 Ⓐ Ⓑ Ⓒ Ⓓ | 85 Ⓐ Ⓑ Ⓒ Ⓓ |
| 14 Ⓐ Ⓑ Ⓒ Ⓓ | 32 Ⓐ Ⓑ Ⓒ Ⓓ | 50 Ⓐ Ⓑ Ⓒ Ⓓ | 68 Ⓐ Ⓑ Ⓒ Ⓓ | 86 Ⓐ Ⓑ Ⓒ Ⓓ |
| 15 Ⓐ Ⓑ Ⓒ Ⓓ | 33 Ⓐ Ⓑ Ⓒ Ⓓ | 51 Ⓐ Ⓑ Ⓒ Ⓓ | 69 Ⓐ Ⓑ Ⓒ Ⓓ | 87 Ⓐ Ⓑ Ⓒ Ⓓ |
| 16 Ⓐ Ⓑ Ⓒ Ⓓ | 34 Ⓐ Ⓑ Ⓒ Ⓓ | 52 Ⓐ Ⓑ Ⓒ Ⓓ | 70 Ⓐ Ⓑ Ⓒ Ⓓ | 88 Ⓐ Ⓑ Ⓒ Ⓓ |
| 17 Ⓐ Ⓑ Ⓒ Ⓓ | 35 Ⓐ Ⓑ Ⓒ Ⓓ | 53 Ⓐ Ⓑ Ⓒ Ⓓ | 71 Ⓐ Ⓑ Ⓒ Ⓓ | 89 Ⓐ Ⓑ Ⓒ Ⓓ |
| 18 Ⓐ Ⓑ Ⓒ Ⓓ | 36 Ⓐ Ⓑ Ⓒ Ⓓ | 54 Ⓐ Ⓑ Ⓒ Ⓓ | 72 Ⓐ Ⓑ Ⓒ Ⓓ | 90 Ⓐ Ⓑ Ⓒ Ⓓ |

# SAMPLE ANSWER SHEET
# FOR SAMPLE PRACTICE EXAMINATION V

| | | | |
|---|---|---|---|
| 1 Ⓣ Ⓕ | 26 Ⓣ Ⓕ | 51 Ⓣ Ⓕ | 76 Ⓣ Ⓕ |
| 2 Ⓣ Ⓕ | 27 Ⓣ Ⓕ | 52 Ⓣ Ⓕ | 77 Ⓣ Ⓕ |
| 3 Ⓣ Ⓕ | 28 Ⓣ Ⓕ | 53 Ⓣ Ⓕ | 78 Ⓣ Ⓕ |
| 4 Ⓣ Ⓕ | 29 Ⓣ Ⓕ | 54 Ⓣ Ⓕ | 79 Ⓣ Ⓕ |
| 5 Ⓣ Ⓕ | 30 Ⓣ Ⓕ | 55 Ⓣ Ⓕ | 80 Ⓣ Ⓕ |
| 6 Ⓣ Ⓕ | 31 Ⓣ Ⓕ | 56 Ⓣ Ⓕ | 81 Ⓣ Ⓕ |
| 7 Ⓣ Ⓕ | 32 Ⓣ Ⓕ | 57 Ⓣ Ⓕ | 82 Ⓣ Ⓕ |
| 8 Ⓣ Ⓕ | 33 Ⓣ Ⓕ | 58 Ⓣ Ⓕ | 83 Ⓣ Ⓕ |
| 9 Ⓣ Ⓕ | 34 Ⓣ Ⓕ | 59 Ⓣ Ⓕ | 84 Ⓣ Ⓕ |
| 10 Ⓣ Ⓕ | 35 Ⓣ Ⓕ | 60 Ⓣ Ⓕ | 85 Ⓣ Ⓕ |
| 11 Ⓣ Ⓕ | 36 Ⓣ Ⓕ | 61 Ⓣ Ⓕ | 86 Ⓣ Ⓕ |
| 12 Ⓣ Ⓕ | 37 Ⓣ Ⓕ | 62 Ⓣ Ⓕ | 87 Ⓣ Ⓕ |
| 13 Ⓣ Ⓕ | 38 Ⓣ Ⓕ | 63 Ⓣ Ⓕ | 88 Ⓣ Ⓕ |
| 14 Ⓣ Ⓕ | 39 Ⓣ Ⓕ | 64 Ⓣ Ⓕ | 89 Ⓣ Ⓕ |
| 15 Ⓣ Ⓕ | 40 Ⓣ Ⓕ | 65 Ⓣ Ⓕ | 90 Ⓣ Ⓕ |
| 16 Ⓣ Ⓕ | 41 Ⓣ Ⓕ | 66 Ⓣ Ⓕ | 91 Ⓣ Ⓕ |
| 17 Ⓣ Ⓕ | 42 Ⓣ Ⓕ | 67 Ⓣ Ⓕ | 92 Ⓣ Ⓕ |
| 18 Ⓣ Ⓕ | 43 Ⓣ Ⓕ | 68 Ⓣ Ⓕ | 93 Ⓣ Ⓕ |
| 19 Ⓣ Ⓕ | 44 Ⓣ Ⓕ | 69 Ⓣ Ⓕ | 94 Ⓣ Ⓕ |
| 20 Ⓣ Ⓕ | 45 Ⓣ Ⓕ | 70 Ⓣ Ⓕ | 95 Ⓣ Ⓕ |
| 21 Ⓣ Ⓕ | 46 Ⓣ Ⓕ | 71 Ⓣ Ⓕ | 96 Ⓣ Ⓕ |
| 22 Ⓣ Ⓕ | 47 Ⓣ Ⓕ | 72 Ⓣ Ⓕ | 97 Ⓣ Ⓕ |
| 23 Ⓣ Ⓕ | 48 Ⓣ Ⓕ | 73 Ⓣ Ⓕ | 98 Ⓣ Ⓕ |
| 24 Ⓣ Ⓕ | 49 Ⓣ Ⓕ | 74 Ⓣ Ⓕ | 99 Ⓣ Ⓕ |
| 25 Ⓣ Ⓕ | 50 Ⓣ Ⓕ | 75 Ⓣ Ⓕ | 100 Ⓣ Ⓕ |

# SAMPLE ANSWER SHEET
# FOR SAMPLE PRACTICE EXAMINATION VI

| | | | |
|---|---|---|---|
| 1 Ⓣ Ⓕ | 26 Ⓣ Ⓕ | 51 Ⓣ Ⓕ | 76 Ⓣ Ⓕ |
| 2 Ⓣ Ⓕ | 27 Ⓣ Ⓕ | 52 Ⓣ Ⓕ | 77 Ⓣ Ⓕ |
| 3 Ⓣ Ⓕ | 28 Ⓣ Ⓕ | 53 Ⓣ Ⓕ | 78 Ⓣ Ⓕ |
| 4 Ⓣ Ⓕ | 29 Ⓣ Ⓕ | 54 Ⓣ Ⓕ | 79 Ⓣ Ⓕ |
| 5 Ⓣ Ⓕ | 30 Ⓣ Ⓕ | 55 Ⓣ Ⓕ | 80 Ⓣ Ⓕ |
| 6 Ⓣ Ⓕ | 31 Ⓣ Ⓕ | 56 Ⓣ Ⓕ | 81 Ⓣ Ⓕ |
| 7 Ⓣ Ⓕ | 32 Ⓣ Ⓕ | 57 Ⓣ Ⓕ | 82 Ⓣ Ⓕ |
| 8 Ⓣ Ⓕ | 33 Ⓣ Ⓕ | 58 Ⓣ Ⓕ | 83 Ⓣ Ⓕ |
| 9 Ⓣ Ⓕ | 34 Ⓣ Ⓕ | 59 Ⓣ Ⓕ | 84 Ⓣ Ⓕ |
| 10 Ⓣ Ⓕ | 35 Ⓣ Ⓕ | 60 Ⓣ Ⓕ | 85 Ⓣ Ⓕ |
| 11 Ⓣ Ⓕ | 36 Ⓣ Ⓕ | 61 Ⓣ Ⓕ | 86 Ⓣ Ⓕ |
| 12 Ⓣ Ⓕ | 37 Ⓣ Ⓕ | 62 Ⓣ Ⓕ | 87 Ⓣ Ⓕ |
| 13 Ⓣ Ⓕ | 38 Ⓣ Ⓕ | 63 Ⓣ Ⓕ | 88 Ⓣ Ⓕ |
| 14 Ⓣ Ⓕ | 39 Ⓣ Ⓕ | 64 Ⓣ Ⓕ | 89 Ⓣ Ⓕ |
| 15 Ⓣ Ⓕ | 40 Ⓣ Ⓕ | 65 Ⓣ Ⓕ | 90 Ⓣ Ⓕ |
| 16 Ⓣ Ⓕ | 41 Ⓣ Ⓕ | 66 Ⓣ Ⓕ | 91 Ⓣ Ⓕ |
| 17 Ⓣ Ⓕ | 42 Ⓣ Ⓕ | 67 Ⓣ Ⓕ | 92 Ⓣ Ⓕ |
| 18 Ⓣ Ⓕ | 43 Ⓣ Ⓕ | 68 Ⓣ Ⓕ | 93 Ⓣ Ⓕ |
| 19 Ⓣ Ⓕ | 44 Ⓣ Ⓕ | 69 Ⓣ Ⓕ | 94 Ⓣ Ⓕ |
| 20 Ⓣ Ⓕ | 45 Ⓣ Ⓕ | 70 Ⓣ Ⓕ | 95 Ⓣ Ⓕ |
| 21 Ⓣ Ⓕ | 46 Ⓣ Ⓕ | 71 Ⓣ Ⓕ | 96 Ⓣ Ⓕ |
| 22 Ⓣ Ⓕ | 47 Ⓣ Ⓕ | 72 Ⓣ Ⓕ | 97 Ⓣ Ⓕ |
| 23 Ⓣ Ⓕ | 48 Ⓣ Ⓕ | 73 Ⓣ Ⓕ | 98 Ⓣ Ⓕ |
| 24 Ⓣ Ⓕ | 49 Ⓣ Ⓕ | 74 Ⓣ Ⓕ | 99 Ⓣ Ⓕ |
| 25 Ⓣ Ⓕ | 50 Ⓣ Ⓕ | 75 Ⓣ Ⓕ | 100 Ⓣ Ⓕ |

# SAMPLE ANSWER SHEET
# FOR SAMPLE PRACTICE EXAMINATION VII

| | | | |
|---|---|---|---|
| 1 Ⓣ Ⓕ | 26 Ⓣ Ⓕ | 51 Ⓣ Ⓕ | 76 Ⓣ Ⓕ |
| 2 Ⓣ Ⓕ | 27 Ⓣ Ⓕ | 52 Ⓣ Ⓕ | 77 Ⓣ Ⓕ |
| 3 Ⓣ Ⓕ | 28 Ⓣ Ⓕ | 53 Ⓣ Ⓕ | 78 Ⓣ Ⓕ |
| 4 Ⓣ Ⓕ | 29 Ⓣ Ⓕ | 54 Ⓣ Ⓕ | 79 Ⓣ Ⓕ |
| 5 Ⓣ Ⓕ | 30 Ⓣ Ⓕ | 55 Ⓣ Ⓕ | 80 Ⓣ Ⓕ |
| 6 Ⓣ Ⓕ | 31 Ⓣ Ⓕ | 56 Ⓣ Ⓕ | 81 Ⓣ Ⓕ |
| 7 Ⓣ Ⓕ | 32 Ⓣ Ⓕ | 57 Ⓣ Ⓕ | 82 Ⓣ Ⓕ |
| 8 Ⓣ Ⓕ | 33 Ⓣ Ⓕ | 58 Ⓣ Ⓕ | 83 Ⓣ Ⓕ |
| 9 Ⓣ Ⓕ | 34 Ⓣ Ⓕ | 59 Ⓣ Ⓕ | 84 Ⓣ Ⓕ |
| 10 Ⓣ Ⓕ | 35 Ⓣ Ⓕ | 60 Ⓣ Ⓕ | 85 Ⓣ Ⓕ |
| 11 Ⓣ Ⓕ | 36 Ⓣ Ⓕ | 61 Ⓣ Ⓕ | 86 Ⓣ Ⓕ |
| 12 Ⓣ Ⓕ | 37 Ⓣ Ⓕ | 62 Ⓣ Ⓕ | 87 Ⓣ Ⓕ |
| 13 Ⓣ Ⓕ | 38 Ⓣ Ⓕ | 63 Ⓣ Ⓕ | 88 Ⓣ Ⓕ |
| 14 Ⓣ Ⓕ | 39 Ⓣ Ⓕ | 64 Ⓣ Ⓕ | 89 Ⓣ Ⓕ |
| 15 Ⓣ Ⓕ | 40 Ⓣ Ⓕ | 65 Ⓣ Ⓕ | 90 Ⓣ Ⓕ |
| 16 Ⓣ Ⓕ | 41 Ⓣ Ⓕ | 66 Ⓣ Ⓕ | 91 Ⓣ Ⓕ |
| 17 Ⓣ Ⓕ | 42 Ⓣ Ⓕ | 67 Ⓣ Ⓕ | 92 Ⓣ Ⓕ |
| 18 Ⓣ Ⓕ | 43 Ⓣ Ⓕ | 68 Ⓣ Ⓕ | 93 Ⓣ Ⓕ |
| 19 Ⓣ Ⓕ | 44 Ⓣ Ⓕ | 69 Ⓣ Ⓕ | 94 Ⓣ Ⓕ |
| 20 Ⓣ Ⓕ | 45 Ⓣ Ⓕ | 70 Ⓣ Ⓕ | 95 Ⓣ Ⓕ |
| 21 Ⓣ Ⓕ | 46 Ⓣ Ⓕ | 71 Ⓣ Ⓕ | 96 Ⓣ Ⓕ |
| 22 Ⓣ Ⓕ | 47 Ⓣ Ⓕ | 72 Ⓣ Ⓕ | 97 Ⓣ Ⓕ |
| 23 Ⓣ Ⓕ | 48 Ⓣ Ⓕ | 73 Ⓣ Ⓕ | 98 Ⓣ Ⓕ |
| 24 Ⓣ Ⓕ | 49 Ⓣ Ⓕ | 74 Ⓣ Ⓕ | 99 Ⓣ Ⓕ |
| 25 Ⓣ Ⓕ | 50 Ⓣ Ⓕ | 75 Ⓣ Ⓕ | 100 Ⓣ Ⓕ |

# SAMPLE ANSWER SHEET
# FOR SAMPLE PRACTICE EXAMINATION VIII

| | | | |
|---|---|---|---|
| 1 Ⓣ Ⓕ | 26 Ⓣ Ⓕ | 51 Ⓐ Ⓑ Ⓒ Ⓓ | 76 Ⓣ Ⓕ |
| 2 Ⓣ Ⓕ | 27 Ⓣ Ⓕ | 52 Ⓐ Ⓑ Ⓒ Ⓓ | 77 Ⓣ Ⓕ |
| 3 Ⓣ Ⓕ | 28 Ⓣ Ⓕ | 53 Ⓐ Ⓑ Ⓒ Ⓓ | 78 Ⓣ Ⓕ |
| 4 Ⓣ Ⓕ | 29 Ⓣ Ⓕ | 54 Ⓐ Ⓑ Ⓒ Ⓓ | 79 Ⓣ Ⓕ |
| 5 Ⓣ Ⓕ | 30 Ⓣ Ⓕ | 55 Ⓐ Ⓑ Ⓒ Ⓓ | 80 Ⓣ Ⓕ |
| 6 Ⓣ Ⓕ | 31 Ⓣ Ⓕ | 56 Ⓐ Ⓑ | 81 Ⓣ Ⓕ |
| 7 Ⓣ Ⓕ | 32 Ⓣ Ⓕ | 57 Ⓐ Ⓑ | 82 Ⓐ Ⓑ |
| 8 Ⓣ Ⓕ | 33 Ⓣ Ⓕ | 58 Ⓐ Ⓑ | 83 Ⓐ Ⓑ |
| 9 Ⓣ Ⓕ | 34 Ⓣ Ⓕ | 59 Ⓐ Ⓑ | 84 Ⓐ Ⓑ |
| 10 Ⓣ Ⓕ | 35 Ⓣ Ⓕ | 60 Ⓐ Ⓑ | 85 Ⓐ Ⓑ |
| 11 Ⓣ Ⓕ | 36 Ⓣ Ⓕ | 61 Ⓐ Ⓑ | 86 Ⓐ Ⓑ |
| 12 Ⓣ Ⓕ | 37 Ⓣ Ⓕ | 62 Ⓐ Ⓑ | 87 Ⓐ Ⓑ |
| 13 Ⓣ Ⓕ | 38 Ⓣ Ⓕ | 63 Ⓐ Ⓑ | 88 Ⓐ Ⓑ |
| 14 Ⓣ Ⓕ | 39 Ⓣ Ⓕ | 64 Ⓐ Ⓑ | 89 Ⓐ Ⓑ |
| 15 Ⓣ Ⓕ | 40 Ⓣ Ⓕ | 65 Ⓐ Ⓑ | 90 Ⓐ Ⓑ |
| 16 Ⓣ Ⓕ | 41 Ⓣ Ⓕ | 66 Ⓐ Ⓑ | 91 Ⓐ Ⓑ |
| 17 Ⓣ Ⓕ | 42 Ⓣ Ⓕ | 67 Ⓐ Ⓑ | 92 Ⓐ Ⓑ |
| 18 Ⓣ Ⓕ | 43 Ⓣ Ⓕ | 68 Ⓐ Ⓑ | 93 Ⓐ Ⓑ Ⓒ Ⓓ |
| 19 Ⓣ Ⓕ | 44 Ⓣ Ⓕ | 69 Ⓐ Ⓑ | 94 Ⓐ Ⓑ Ⓒ Ⓓ |
| 20 Ⓣ Ⓕ | 45 Ⓣ Ⓕ | 70 Ⓐ Ⓑ | 95 Ⓐ Ⓑ Ⓒ Ⓓ |
| 21 Ⓣ Ⓕ | 46 Ⓣ Ⓕ | 71 Ⓐ Ⓑ | 96 Ⓐ Ⓑ Ⓒ Ⓓ |
| 22 Ⓣ Ⓕ | 47 Ⓣ Ⓕ | 72 Ⓐ Ⓑ | 97 Ⓐ Ⓑ Ⓒ Ⓓ |
| 23 Ⓣ Ⓕ | 48 Ⓣ Ⓕ | 73 Ⓐ Ⓑ | 98 Ⓐ Ⓑ Ⓒ Ⓓ |
| 24 Ⓣ Ⓕ | 49 Ⓣ Ⓕ | 74 Ⓐ Ⓑ | 99 Ⓐ Ⓑ Ⓒ Ⓓ |
| 25 Ⓣ Ⓕ | 50 Ⓣ Ⓕ | 75 Ⓐ Ⓑ | 100 Ⓐ Ⓑ Ⓒ Ⓓ |

# SAMPLE PRACTICE EXAMINATION I

DIRECTIONS FOR ANSWERING QUESTIONS

Each question has four suggested answers, lettered A, B, C, and D. Decide which one is the best answer, locate the question number on the sample answer sheet, and darken the area with a soft pencil which corresponds to the answer that you have selected.

The time allowed for the entire examination is 3 hours.

1. What is a mulch?

   (A) a fertilizer high in nitrogen
   (B) a material spread upon the surface of the soil to conserve moisture and inhibit weed growth
   (C) a chemical compound sprayed on the foliage of plants to prevent wilting
   (D) a mixture of coarse gravel, stones, and broken rock used for drainage in the bottom of flower pots and planting tubs

2. A good permanent grass seed mixture for a dry, shady lawn area is

   (A) 2 parts Merion bluegrass, 1 part Kentucky bluegrass
   (B) 1 part Merion bluegrass, 2 parts Rhode Island or Colonial bent grass
   (C) 1 part chewing fescue, 1 part Illahee fescue, 1 part Pennlawn fescue
   (D) 2 parts Perennial ryegrass, 1 part Italian ryegrass

3. Which of the following is the best cutting height for the average lawn in the New York City area in

hot weather?

(A) 1/4"
(B) 1/2"
(C) 1"
(D) 2"

4. Earthworms are most likely to

(A) make good soil from poor soil
(B) make good soil into even better soil
(C) ruin good soil
(D) indicate a lack of organic matter in the soil

5. Before turning over a power rotary lawn mower to clean the underside and cutting blade you should

(A) adjust the carburetor idle setting to low speed
(B) allow the engine to cool for at least 10 minutes
(C) remove the high-tension wire from the spark plug
(D) adjust the carburetor setting to full choke

6. A 10-6-4 fertilizer contains

(A) 4% nitrogen
(B) 10% potassium
(C) 6% potassium
(D) 6% phosphorus

7. Which of the following is generally the best pH range for a lawn soil?

(A) pH 2 - 3.5
(B) pH 3 - 4.5
(C) pH 6 - 6.5
(D) pH 8 - 10.5

8. Peat moss is best used as

(A) a mulch
(B) an organic soil amendment
(C) a fertilizer
(D) a substitute for lime

9. What does pH indicate?

(A) the amount of nitrogen in the soil
(B) the amount of moisture in the soil
(C) the acidity or alkalinity of the soil
(D) the amount of organic matter in the soil

10. In order to promote dense growth on all parts of a hedge, it is best to prune it so that the

(A) top is wider than the bottom

(B) bottom is wider than the top
(C) top and bottom are of equal width
(D) top and bottom are narrower than the middle

11. When should shrubs that bloom in the spring such as weigela and lilac generally be pruned?

(A) as soon as they are finished blooming
(B) just before they bloom
(C) while they are blooming
(D) when they are still dormant

12. Assume that you wish to cut a large limb off a tree trunk. In order to do this without damaging the tree, the minimum number of separate saw cuts that should usually be made is

(A) 1
(B) 2
(C) 3
(D) 4

13. The best method of controlling infestations of scale insects on young trees is by

(A) dusting the trees with a good fungicide
(B) removing and burning affected limbs and branches
(C) digging up and destroying the trees
(D) spraying the trees with dormant oil

14. In a slat house for shading plants, the direction in which the roof slats should run is

(A) an east-west direction
(B) a north-south direction
(C) a northeast by southwest direction
(D) a northwest by southeast direction

15. Which one of the following plants is a monocotyledon?

(A) begonia
(B) geranium
(C) phlox
(D) iris

16. You are in charge of a small lawn area of 1850 sq. ft. You are asked to apply lime on this lawn at the rate of 46 lbs. per 1000 sq. ft. The number of lbs. of lime you will need to cover the entire area of the lawn is most nearly

(A) 85
(B) 86
(C) 87
(D) 89

17. A Kentucky bluegrass lawn requires 3 lbs. of actual nitrogen per 1000 sq. ft. How many lbs. of 10-6-4 fertilizer will be needed to fertilize a 5000 sq. ft. lawn of Kentucky bluegrass?

(A) 15.5
(B) 150
(C) 555
(D) 50

18. You need to fill a 32 oz. bottle with a solution containing 10% malathion, but all you have is a gallon of 50% malathion solution. How many oz. of the 50% malathion solution and how many oz. of water should you put in the bottle?

(A) 3.2 oz. of 50% malathion solution and 28.8 oz. of water
(B) 6.4 oz. of 50% malathion solution and 25.6 oz. of water
(C) 9.6 oz. of 50% malathion solution and 22.4 oz. of water
(D) 12.8 oz. of 50% malathion solution and 19.2 oz. of water

19. The term "hardiness" is most often used to refer to the

(A) tensile strength of a plant's stem and branches
(B) ability of plants to endure low temperatures
(C) amount of wind force a plant can withstand
(D) length of time a plant can survive without water

20. Which one of the following is <u>not</u> a method of plant propagation?

(A) layering
(B) budding
(C) chlorosis
(D) division

21. Clematis, wisteria, and ampelopsis are all

(A) indoor foliage plants
(B) outdoor annuals
(C) grown from bulbs planted each fall
(D) ornamental climbing plants

22. When attaching a scion to a stock you should use which one of the following methods?

(A) whip or tongue
(B) tack weld
(C) pintle and gudgeon
(D) clinch or rivet and burr

23. "Pinching" as performed by a gardener is a method of

    (A) grafting
    (B) pruning
    (C) propagation
    (D) pollination

24. In a project involving the laying of sod, the soil was properly cultivated, fertilized, and the turf laid and rolled in the approved fashion. Water was periodically applied in ample quantity. After a few days the grass began to die around the edges of each rectangular piece of sod. The best method of avoiding such a problem is probably to

    (A) add more fertilizer to the soil before the turf is laid
    (B) apply lime before and after the sod has been laid
    (C) brush a dressing of sandy loam into the joints between the sods
    (D) water the sod only in bright sunlight

25. A label on a plant was marked as follows:

    Abies nobilis glauca
    Pinaceae

    The name of this plant reveals that

    (A) the species is Abies, the genus is nobilis, the family is glauca, and the variety is Pinaceae
    (B) the family is Abies, the variety is nobilis, the genus is glauca, and the species is Pinaceae
    (C) the genus is Abies, the family is nobilis, the species is glauca, and the variety is Pinaceae
    (D) the genus is Abies, the species is nobilis, the variety is glauca, and the family is Pinaceae

26. A small deciduous tree in leaf has just been dug from the ground, transplanted into a tub, and then watered until the soil is saturated. It quickly shows symptoms of severe wilting. In trying to save this tree, which of the following would be the <u>least</u> acceptable remedy?

    (A) Remove some of the foliage, either by removing some of the leaves or some of the smaller branches with their foliage
    (B) Wet the plant's foliage, place a plastic bag over the entire tree, and place it either in a shady place or a darkened room

(C) Remove the tree from the tub, remove all the soil from the roots, and then place the plant in a pail of water so the roots are completely submerged
(D) Place the tree under the constant mist of a fine spray

27. A certain broad-leaf evergreen tree had many flowers in the spring, but bore no fruit in the fall. The next spring a close examination of the flowers revealed only stamens and no pistils. The probable reason for the failure of the tree to fruit is that the

(A) flowers were deformed
(B) tree was a male
(C) tree was a female and there was no male in the vicinity
(D) tree was planted too far north and the cold weather prevented it from fruiting

28. Which one of the following trees would be least desirable for planting in a shady area?

(A) dogwood
(B) pine
(C) hemlock
(D) holly

29. Brown patches are noticed in a sunny lawn area in the summer. A close examination reveals numerous brown insects around the grass roots in the patches about 1/6" long with white markings on their backs. These insects most likely are

(A) aphids
(B) scale insects
(C) chinch bugs
(D) leaf hoppers

30. Many diseases of lawn grasses can be treated effectively with

(A) benomyl (benlate)
(B) 2,4-D
(C) DDT
(D) rotenone

31. Of the following the best way to reduce the acidity of soil is to apply

(A) limestone
(B) flowers of sulfur
(C) aluminum sulfate
(D) water

32. The most effective of the following actions to stop erosion of soil on steep embankments is to

    (A) break the flow of water on the embankment
    (B) dig several water channels from the top of the embankment to the bottom
    (C) rototill the embankment
    (D) spray the embankment with 2,4-D

33. A complete fertilizer contains

    (A) nitrogen, phosphorus, and iron
    (B) calcium, potassium, and sulfur
    (C) nitrogen, phosphorus, and potassium
    (D) calcium, carbon, and nitrogen

34. Plants produce seeds by means of

    (A) pollination and fertilization
    (B) cultivation and grafting
    (C) hybridization and air-layering
    (D) rooting and hydrogenation

35. If a tree is to be replanted in a heavy clay-loam soil with questionable drainage it would be best to plant the tree

    (A) three inches deeper than it was planted before
    (B) six inches deeper than it was planted before
    (C) at the same level as before and back-fill with sand
    (D) slightly higher in the soil than it was planted before

36. Suckers are most likely to develop from

    (A) buds
    (B) roots
    (C) shoots
    (D) leaf cuttings

37. All of the following are piercing-sucking insects <u>except</u>

    (A) white fly
    (B) leaf hopper
    (C) lace bug
    (D) black vine weevil

38. Knowing and using good horticultural books for reference is important in gardening work. Which of the following is a good horticultural book?

(A) Hortus Second by Liberty Hyde Bailey
(B) Plant Location in Theory and in Practice by Melvin Greenhut
(C) How Green Was My Valley by Richard Llewellyn
(D) The Greening of America by Charles Reich

39. The pine bark aphid is a pest of pines such as the Eastern White Pine (Pinus strobus). A superior-type emulsifiable oil spray can be applied during the early spring when the tree is still dormant. Which of the following conditions are best for applying the spray?

(A) there is no wind, the day temperature is 50°F. or higher, the night temperature above the mid 30s, no rain predicted
(B) a slight wind is predicted, the day temperature does not exceed 48°F., the night temperature is predicted to fall below freezing
(C) a slight wind is predicted, the day temperature and the night temperature are both above 85°F., and the day is misty
(D) the aphids start to move

40. An excellent fungicide which not only has historical significance but is still highly recommended for control of certain fungus diseases contains copper sulfate, hydrated lime, and water. This fungicide is called

(A) ferbam
(B) bordeaux mixture
(C) solution C.S.H.L.
(D) captan

41. A heavy mulch is least desirable for

(A) iris
(B) rhododendrons
(C) azaleas
(D) newly planted trees

42. You have noticed that a number of older needles fall each year from a pine tree. This phenomenon is probably due to

(A) root rot
(B) insufficient fertilizer

(C) natural aging of the needles
(D) insufficient water

43. The best time to sow grass seed in New York City is

(A) mid-August to mid-September
(B) mid-March to mid-April
(C) late April to mid-May
(D) late May to early June

44. In order to maintain natural growth, the best of the following methods of pruning forsythia is to remove

(A) half of the top growth
(B) only the apical buds
(C) up to one-third of the older stems
(D) all growth over two feet

45. Which one of the following trees can be safely pruned in spring when sap is flowing?

(A) acer saccharium - sugar maple
(B) ulmus species - elms
(C) cladrastis lutea - yellowwood
(D) pinus thumbergii - japanese black pine

46. Of the following the best way to treat trees or shrubs with dead and diseased branches is to

(A) leave them alone
(B) prune to remove 1/3 of older wood
(C) prune back to healthy wood
(D) spray with 2,4-D

47. Anthracnose disease of platanus species (plane trees) is more prevalent in wet spring weather. This disease is caused by a

(A) beetle
(B) fungus
(C) mildew
(D) gas leak

48. Peat moss is frequently used in gardening to change soil conditions. Which of the following is the best definition of peat moss?

(A) a short, slow-growing plant
(B) completely decomposed animal life
(C) partially decomposed plant life
(D) a type of wood

49. A sprayer that has been used to spray insecticides and will be used for this purpose in the future should never be used to apply

(A) fungicides
(B) miticides
(C) malathion
(D) herbicides

50. It is especially important that an excess of fertilizer not be applied to the soil because of the possibility of root damage. This is due to the fact that fertilizer is

(A) an acid
(B) a base
(C) a salt
(D) an alkali

51. Of the following, the best time to apply fertilizer to lawn grasses is usually when the

(A) soil is moist and the grass is wet
(B) grass is dry and the soil is moist
(C) soil and the grass are dry
(D) soil is dry and the grass is wet

52. Assume that a child's rope swing has been attached to a tree by tying the rope securely around the lowest limb. Of the following it is most important that

(A) girdling of the limb at the point of attachment of the rope does not eventually occur
(B) only a natural fiber rope is used
(C) the rope be lengthened as the tree grows in height
(D) as the limb grows in length the swing be moved back toward the trunk to adjust for linear growth

53. An established lawn that requires watering during dry periods should be watered

(A) lightly twice a day in the morning and again at dusk
(B) lightly once a day in the morning unless the humidity is above 90%
(C) thoroughly to a depth of at least 4 inches early in the day
(D) thoroughly to a depth of 4 inches in the morning and again at dusk

54. A rhododendron shows severe yellowing of leaves. The problem is due to an iron deficiency. To cor-

rect this, it is most effective to apply

(A) iron carbide
(B) iron pyrites
(C) iron chelate
(D) iron oxide

55. The color of the flower of some species of plants is distinctly affected by soil alkalinity or acidity as well as the amount of aluminum or iron in the soil. When the soil is neutral or alkaline the flower color is pinker, whereas under acid soil conditions the flower color is bluer. Which one of the following plants is best known to exhibit this response?

(A) rosa species - Roses
(B) hydrangea macrophylla (hortensis) - house hydrangea
(C) chrysanthemum morifolium - florist and garden chrysanthemums
(D) begonia semperflorens - wax or fibrous-rooted begonias

56. Which one of the following terms refers to a method in which trees or shrubs can be trained into a special shape or form?

(A) abscission
(B) layering
(C) pricking-out
(D) espalier

57. Which one of the following is <u>not</u> a shrub?

(A) pieris japonica
(B) abelia grandiflora
(C) acer platanoides
(D) viburnum japonicum

58. A new method for accounting for the time gardeners spend on each job has been implemented. The gardeners object to the new method, complaining to the supervisor that the previous method was superior. Of the following the best action for the supervisor to take first is to

(A) find out specifically to what your crew objects
(B) suggest to your crew members that they are correct and that management does not really understand the effect of the change
(C) tell your crew to try the new method and that if they still feel that way in a few weeks they can go back to the old method
(D) take a vote among your crew to determine which method to use

59. For the supervisor to complain about working conditions is

(A) advisable, since it makes him "one of the boys"
(B) advisable, since it allows him to get his feelings out in the open
(C) inadvisable, since it permits the crew to depend on the attitudes and approval of their supervisor
(D) inadvisable, since it brings attention to problems but does not resolve them

60. For a supervisor to ask subordinates for their suggestions on better gardening methods is

(A) inadvisable; they may feel that she lacks self-confidence
(B) inadvisable; it is poor practice to become too friendly with subordinates
(C) advisable; it makes workers feel they have a hand in decision-making
(D) advisable; those who make the suggestions can be held responsible for results

61. For the supervisor to explain agency objectives for the year ahead to a new employee is

(A) inadvisable; the new employee may leave before the year is up
(B) inadvisable; the new employee has nothing to do with the goals of the department
(C) advisable; it may enable the new employee to do the job with less training
(D) advisable; it may give the new employee a sense of personal involvement and motivation

62. When a new gardener reports for duty for the first time, which of the following should be discussed with her first?

(A) departmental rules and regulations that relate to her employment
(B) the priorities that she should assign to her work
(C) the latest techniques of getting the technical work done
(D) the recognition of what constitutes an error in her work and its consequences

63. While you are trimming shrubs in the park, a woman comes up and tells you that her civic club is running a benefit for the handicapped and that it would be wonderful if the Parks Department would

donate some flowers to this worthy cause. You do not know how this type of situation has been handled in the past. Of the following, the best action for you to take is to tell her

(A) you are sure the Parks Department will be happy to donate flowers, and take her name and address
(B) you have nothing to do with Parks Department policy and cannot make that decision
(C) you are not sure what the Parks Department policy is but you think she is wasting her time trying to get flowers from the Parks Department
(D) you are not sure what Parks Department policy is but that you will tell her how to get more information

64. One of the gardeners has made an error in the care of bulbs, resulting in the loss of many expensive bulbs. Of the following, the best way for the supervisor to handle this situation initially is to

(A) write a memo on the care of bulbs and post it where your crew can refer to it
(B) call your crew together and discuss the proper care of bulbs
(C) speak privately to the crew member who made the error and discuss his error and proper care of bulbs with him
(D) tell the crew member who made the error you will not report him at present, but if this type of error occurs again you will recommend his dismissal

65. It has been brought to the attention of the supervisor that several expensive tools are missing from the tool cabinet. Since this had never before been a problem, the cabinet was always left unlocked. Of the following, the best way for the supervisor to handle this situation is to

(A) lock the cabinet, and give keys to all your crew members, making them all responsible for the tools
(B) lock the cabinet, and make one of your crew members responsible for the key to the cabinet and the tools inside
(C) announce to your crew members that if a tool is missing they will all have to be charged an appropriate amount towards the purchase of a new tool
(D) assign each crew member a particular tool and have him use this device exclusively

66. Of the following, the best reason for the practice of requiring gardeners to sign in and out for lunch is that

(A) crew members are more productive when more strictly controlled
(B) it enables the supervisor to regulate the time and working hours of the crew members more directly
(C) it prevents crew members from leaving the work area during their lunch period
(D) the supervisor will find out the preferred lunch period of each individual crew member

67. While pruning shrubs, a gardener trips over what she thinks was a loose cobblestone. After checking to make sure she has suffered no injury, of the following the most advisable action for the supervisor to take next is to

(A) tell her to be more careful in the future
(B) determine what actually caused the accident
(C) post safety rules where they can be seen by all gardeners
(D) assign her to a different type of work at another location

68. One of the gardeners advises his supervisor that the lawn mower he has been using has just broken down. Of the following, the best reason for the supervisor to try to operate the mower himself is to

(A) test the worker's knowledge with his performance on the job
(B) keep the machines in need of repair in service as long as possible
(C) show that supervisors can do the work of the crew members
(D) determine whether a minor adjustment will bring the machine to operating condition

69. A supervisor has just explained to her most competent gardener a root-pruning procedure that she wishes him to follow. The gardener tells the supervisor that he is a little uncertain about it and is not sure he can handle it. Of the following, the best action for the supervisor to take is to

(A) show the gardener how much confidence she has in him by leaving him alone to do the job
(B) have another gardener work with him to make sure that the job is done correctly

(C) stay with him while he does the job to make sure that he knows how to do it correctly
(D) drop the assignment until such time as he indicates that he is ready for it

70. While you are replanting flowers, a man comes up and starts berating you for the condition of the park. Of the following, the best way to handle this situation is to

(A) suggest that he write to the Parks Department about his complaints
(B) ask the man to leave and call for a police officer if he does not
(C) explain to the man that those who use the park are primarily responsible for its condition
(D) tell him that his opinions about the condition of the park are wrong

71. Gardeners should be courteous to the public primarily because

(A) someone might report them if they are not
(B) this might earn them a merit increase
(C) a good relationship between the Department and the public is important
(D) this makes for better morale among their crew members

72. A supervisor has been asked to evaluate the performance of one of his gardeners. The one of the following that should be given the <u>least</u> consideration when making this evaluation is the gardener's attitude towards

(A) her co-workers
(B) the organization
(C) her friends
(D) the supervisor

Answer questions 73 through 75 on the basis of the following report.

To: John Greene — Date: May 5, 1984
General Park Foreman

From: Earl Jones — Subject:
Gardener

On May 3, as I was finishing a job six feet from the boathouse, I observed that the hole that had been filled in last week was not level with the ground around it. This seems to be a hazardous condition because it might cause pedestrians to fall into it. I therefore suggest that this job be re-done as soon as possible.

73. This report should be considered poorly written mainly because

    (A) it does not give enough information to take appropriate action
    (B) too many different tenses are used
    (C) it describes no actual personal injury to anyone
    (D) there is no recommendation in the report to remedy the situation

74. It is noted that the subject of the report has been left out. Which of the following statements would be best as the subject of this report?

    (A) observation made by Earl Jones, Gardener
    (B) deteriorating condition of Park grounds
    (C) report of dangerous condition near boathouse
    (D) a dangerous walk through the Park

75. In order for John Greene to take appropriate action, additional information should be added to the report giving the

    (A) exact date the repair was made
    (B) exact location of the hole
    (C) exact time the observation was made
    (D) names of the crew who previously filled in the hole

Questions 76 through 80 are based on the Fact Situation and the Repair Request Report form below. Read the Fact Situation carefully and examine the blank report form. Questions 76 through 80 ask how the report form should be filled in based on the information given in the Fact Situation.

<u>Fact Situation</u>

"John Smith is a gardener permanently assigned to the greenhouse in Queens. On Tuesday morning he arrives at the greenhouse at 8 <u>a.m.</u>, and sees that seven panes of glass in the west wing of the greenhouse have been broken. Since several large rocks are found on the greenhouse floor, it appears that the panes of the windows have been broken by vandals. It is necessary to repair the windows immediately due to the cold weather.

In order to arrange for the repair, John Smith must complete the following Repair Request Report."

REPAIR REQUEST REPORT

1. Date of Request __________ 2. Time ________
3. Location of Needed Repair ____________________
4. Type of Repair Requested ____________________
5. Reason for Request ____________________

______________________________________________

6. Signed ______________ 7. Title ____________
8. Additional Comments ____________________

______________________________________________

76. Which of the following should be entered in blank 4?

    (A) rock removal
    (B) broken glass
    (C) window pane replacement
    (D) heater installation

77. Based on the information given in the Fact Situation, it is impossible to fill in which one of the following blanks?

    (A) blank 1
    (B) blank 3
    (C) blank 5
    (D) blank 7

78. Which of the following would be most appropriate to include in blank 8?

    (A) "John Smith was on time for work on January 10, 1984."
    (B) "It seems that the windows were broken by vandals."
    (C) "The weather forecast for the next few days is unknown."
    (D) "Identity of vandals is unknown."

79. Of the following the best way for John Smith to show his supervisor that the Repair Request Report was

properly filled out is to

(A) personally deliver the Report to the repair crew
(B) have two signatures instead of one required in blank 6
(C) show his supervisor a duplicate copy of the Report
(D) in blank 8 include the dimensions of the panes of glass needed

80. It is necessary to emphasize the need to have the repair made quickly. The proper blank on the form to show the urgency of this request is

(A) blank 2
(B) blank 3
(C) blank 7
(D) blank 8

## Answer Key

| | | | | |
|---|---|---|---|---|
| 1. B | 17. B | 33. C | 49. D | 65. B |
| 2. C | 18. B | 34. A | 50. C | 66. B |
| 3. D | 19. B | 35. D | 51. B | 67. B |
| 4. B | 20. C | 36. A | 52. A | 68. D |
| 5. C | 21. D | 37. D | 53. C | 69. C |
| 6. D | 22. A | 38. A | 54. C | 70. A |
| 7. C | 23. B | 39. A | 55. B | 71. C |
| 8. B | 24. C | 40. B | 56. D | 72. C |
| 9. C | 25. D | 41. A | 57. C | 73. A |
| 10. B | 26. C | 42. C | 58. A | 74. C |
| 11. A | 27. B | 43. A | 59. D | 75. B |
| 12. C | 28. B | 44. C | 60. C | 76. C |
| 13. D | 29. C | 45. D | 61. D | 77. A |
| 14. B | 30. A | 46. C | 62. A | 78. B |
| 15. D | 31. A | 47. B | 63. D | 79. C |
| 16. A | 32. A | 48. C | 64. C | 80. D |

# SAMPLE PRACTICE EXAMINATION II

DIRECTIONS FOR ANSWERING QUESTIONS

Each question has four suggested answers, lettered A, B, C, and D. Decide which one is the best answer, find the question number on the sample answer sheet, and darken the area with a soft pencil which corresponds to the answer you have selected.

The time allowed for the entire examination is 3 hours.

1. For best growth, azaleas require a soil that is

   (A) neutral
   (B) either alkaline or neutral
   (C) alkaline
   (D) acid

Questions 2 to 6 give the names of shrubs. Column I gives suggested times for pruning shrubs. For each shrub in questions 2 to 6, select from Column I the best time to prune.

| | Column I |
|---|---|
| 2. buddleja | (A) prune in spring after flowering |
| 3. common lilac | (B) prune in fall after flowering |
| 4. peegee hydrangea | |
| 5. rose of sharon | |
| 6. vanhoutte's spiraea | |

7. Which of the following is the <u>least</u> acceptable procedure when transplanting trees?

   (A) prune the top back about one fourth
   (B) root prune a large tree for at least one growing season before it is transplanted

(C) transplant in the spring or the fall
(D) transplant only large trees because they can withstand the shock of transplanting better

8. When a deciduous shrub is dug with a ball of earth for transplanting from one location to another, the size of the ball of earth should usually be about

(A) twice the spread of the branches
(B) one-and-one-half times the spread of the branches
(C) equal to the spread of the branches
(D) one-half the spread of the branches

Questions 9 to 12 give the names of 4 pairs of shrubs. Classify each pair of shrubs according to the scheme shown in Column II.

9. mountain laurel - fragrant viburnum
10. mountain andromeda - pfitzer juniper
11. dwarf japanese yew - pyramidal arborvitae
12. sweet mockorange - snowhill hydrangea

Column II

(A) both shrubs are deciduous
(B) both shrubs are evergreen
(C) one shrub is deciduous and one is evergreen

Questions 13 to 17 give the names of 5 shrubs. Classify each shrub according to height as in Column III.

13. shrub althea
14. slender deutzia
15. tartarian honeysuckle
16. japanese andromeda
17. thunberg spires

Column III

(A) low shrub - about 3 feet in height
(B) medium shrub - about 5 feet in height
(C) tall shrub - about 8 feet or more in height

18. Which of the following is true about California privet but <u>not</u> about japanese barberry?

(A) It is suitable for use as a hedge material
(B) It requires little clipping for a neat appearance
(C) It grows very tall
(D) It is thorny

19. Outdoor fall planting is not recommended for

    (A) dahlias
    (B) hyacinths
    (C) lilies-of-the-valley
    (D) tulips

20. A characteristic of annuals is that they usually

    (A) grow well on any soil
    (B) grow well only on considerably acid soil
    (C) are shade-loving
    (D) are sun-loving

21. The recommended spacing between sweet pea plants is

    (A) over 24 inches
    (B) 18 - 24 inches
    (C) 6 - 12 inches
    (D) 1 - 4 inches

22. To say that a seed is <u>viable</u>, means that it

    (A) is subject to fungus disease
    (B) is subject to insect damage
    (C) can take root and grow
    (D) cannot grow in moist soils

Each of questions 23 to 26 gives the name of a mulch that may be classified under one of the headings in Column IV. For each mulch, select the heading from Column IV under which it is most correctly classified.

| | Column IV |
|---|---|
| 23. corn cobs | (A) acid mulch |
| 24. decayed pine needles | (B) non-acid mulch |
| 25. grass clippings | |
| 26. peat moss | |

27. A characteristic of Merion Kentucky bluegrass is that it

    (A) is highly susceptible to leafspot
    (B) needs heavy watering daily
    (C) will thrive on close cutting
    (D) germinates quickly

28. Fertilization of bluegrass and fescue grasses in the summer is

    (A) desirable because the usual dryness of this

season requires increased feeding to offset the shortage of moisture
(B) not desirable because there is more chance of burning the grass
(C) desirable because this is the period of their most active growth
(D) not desirable because they are semi-dormant and fertilization will stimulate weed growth

Questions 29 to 33 give the names of 5 lawn grasses. For each grass, select the statement from Column V that is most applicable.

Column V

29. Kentucky bluegrass
30. red fescue
31. rough bluegrass
32. bent grass
33. Meyer Zoysia

(A) used mainly for golf course putting greens
(B) best grass for sunny places is good soil
(C) suitable for moist, shady areas
(D) turns brown in fall until mid-spring
(E) best grass for dry soil, sun or shade

Each of questions 34 to 37 gives the name of a weed. For each weed, select the best weed killer from Column VI.

Column VI

34. chickweed
35. dandelion
36. plantain
37. speedwells (Veronica)

(A) 2,4-D
(B) 2,4,5-TP (Silver)
(C) endothal

38. Just before seeding a new lawn on average soil, a 5-10-5 fertilizer should be applied at the rate of

(A) 100 lbs. for every 1,000 sq. ft.
(B) 75 lbs. for every 1,000 sq. ft.
(C) 40 lbs. for every 1,000 sq. ft.
(D) 20 lbs. for every 1,000 sq. ft.

Where it is difficult to establish and maintain grass, such as on slopes and in deep shade, the planting of a ground cover is recommended. Questions 39 to 41 give the names of 3 ground cover plants. Select from Column VII the descriptive statement that is most applicable to each.

Column VII

39. english ivy
40. japanese pachysandra
41. myrtle

(A) small, dark green, glossy leaves; violet blue flowers
(B) trailing evergreen vine
(C) spreads by suckers; greenish-white flowers; plants about 8 inches high
(D) a bunch-growing member of the lily family; 8-12 inches high; purple to white flowers

42. Serious and widespread diseases of lawn grasses are caused mostly by

(A) algae
(B) bacteria
(C) crab grass
(D) fungi

43. Anthracnose is a type of

(A) worm
(B) insect pest
(C) lawn grass
(D) fungus disease

Each of questions 44 to 47 gives the name of an insect which may be classified under one of the headings in Column VIII. For each insect, select the heading from Column VIII under which it is most correctly classified.

Column VIII

44. aphid
45. grasshopper
46. lady beetle (ladybug)
47. syrphid fly

(A) insect beneficial to plants
(B) insect injurious to plants
(C) insect neither beneficial nor injurious to plants

Each of questions 48 to 51 gives the name of a fumigant or an insecticide that may be classified under one of the headings in Column IX. For each fumigant or insecticide, select the heading from Column IX under which it is most correctly classified.

48. arsenate of lead
49. chloropicrin
50. pyrethrum
51. rotenone

Column IX

(A) a plant insecticide non-poisonous to man
(B) a plant insecticide poisonous to man
(C) a soil fumigant that should not be used on plants

52. A disadvantage of DDT is that it

(A) is not effective against sucking insects
(B) is not effective against chewing insects
(C) destroys the roots of most flowering plants
(D) destroys the natural enemies of various mites

53. A characteristic of chlordane is that it

(A) does not act as a contact poison
(B) does not act as a stomach poison
(C) has long-lasting effects
(D) is slow-acting

54. For a soil test, it is best to dig the samples of soil in the

(A) early spring
(B) summer
(C) early fall
(D) winter

55. The symbol used to indicate soil acidity is

(A) AC
(B) Hp
(C) pH
(D) SA

56. Loam is a type of soil that

(A) contains no organic matter
(B) is coarser than clay
(C) is coarser than sand
(D) is usually infertile

57. A poor way to improve the structure of a sandy soil is to add

(A) compost
(B) humus
(C) organic matter
(D) sand

58. As compared to a sandy soil, a characteristic of a clay soil is that it

(A) able to hold less water
(B) harder to work when wet
(C) quicker to dry out in the spring
(D) quicker to warm up in the spring

59. A characteristic of compost is that it

(A) decreases slightly the amount of plant nutrient in the soil
(B) decreases slightly the humus content of the soil
(C) improves soil texture in flower gardens
(D) is naturally free of weed seeds

60. An advantage of a commercial fertilizer over an animal manure is that a commercial fertilizer

(A) has a higher percentage of plant nutrients
(B) adds to the organic content of the soil
(C) greatly increases bacterial activity in the soil
(D) will not burn plant roots

61. A disadvantage of using raw bone meal as a fertilizer is that

(A) it increases the soil acidity over a period of years
(B) it is unsafe for use on most plants
(C) its nitrogen content is very slowly available to plants
(D) its phosphorus content is very slowly available to plants

62. What is the action of superphosphate applied to the soil as a top dressing?

(A) It does not penetrate the soil
(B) It penetrates the soil very slowly
(C) It penetrates the soil moderately fast
(D) It penetrates the soil very quickly

63. The addition of which one of the following will be likely to make the soil more acid?

(A) aluminum sulphate
(B) lime
(C) oak leafmold
(D) sawdust

64. Which one of the following is <u>not</u> alkaline in its reaction?

(A) ammonium phosphate
(B) calcium nitrate
(C) cyanamide
(D) wood ashes

65. Which one of these statements about a 4-12-4 fertilizer is true?

(A) The first number shows the percentage of phosphorus
(B) The first number shows the percentage of potassium
(C) The last number shows the percentage of potash
(D) The second number shows the percentage of nitrogen

66. A good <u>organic</u> source of nitrogen is

(A) ammonium sulphate
(B) nitrate of soda
(C) bone meal
(D) dried blood

67. The one of the following that is <u>not</u> a source of potash is

(A) steamed bone meal
(B) wood ashes
(C) potassium chloride
(D) potassium sulphate

68. Urea is a form of

(A) iron
(B) nitrogen
(C) phosphorus
(D) potassium

69. To hold an electric hedge cutter with both hands when using it is considered

(A) good procedure because it lessens the severity of electric shocks
(B) poor procedure because it increases the likelihood of receiving electric shocks
(C) good procedure because it reduces the chance of an accident
(D) poor procedure because it slows up the work

70. Reel power mowers as contrasted with rotary power mowers

(A) are easier to control
(B) cause fewer accidents
(C) cost less
(D) cut closer to trees

71. A gardener stands a 24 ft. ladder against an upright tree trunk. To safely use the ladder, the distance between the base of the tree trunk and the foot of the ladder should be approximately

(A) 8 inches
(B) 2 feet
(C) 3 feet
(D) 6 feet

72. Compared with the hydraulic sprayer, the mist blower

(A) causes more loss of spray material from dripping
(B) is always preferred in areas inaccessible to heavy equipment
(C) is less affected by windy weather
(D) requires greater skill by the operator

73. A supervisor notices that one of his gardeners does not get along with the rest of the gardeners. The best thing for the supervisor to do would be to

(A) ignore the situation since it probably won't affect work output
(B) tell his workers they must get along with each other if they don't want to be transferred
(C) try to find the reason for the trouble to see if the differences can be settled
(D) write a report to his superior and await instructions

74. A gardener supervising a group of gardeners on a work project spoke to them one morning just before lunch about the importance of getting back to work on time after lunch. He turned to one of them and said, "Bill, you have been particularly guilty of coming back late from lunch." The gardener's action was <u>not</u> good because

(A) he could have taken care of the problem better and with less waste of time by issuing a written order to them
(B) he should have named at least one other man who was guilty of this violation

(C) he should not have criticized him in front of the others
(D) this was not a proper subject to talk about at a group meeting

75. Suppose that as a supervisor you are in charge of several gardeners. Warning them that they will be penalized if they do poor work is

(A) good practice because it is only fair that they know what the penalties are for neglect of duty
(B) poor practice because then you will actually have to penalize them if they don't do good work
(C) good practice because they will try to do better work
(D) poor practice because they should be encouraged to do good work without such warnings

76. If you are training a new member of your crew to use a piece of equipment, it would probably be <u>least</u> important for you to

(A) give her a set of written instructions on use of the equipment
(B) give her an actual demonstration in using the equipment
(C) watch her using the equipment the first time
(D) check her frequently to see how she is progressing

77. Your supervisor gives you a letter of complaint from a citizen and tells you to "look into this and get the facts." It would be a good idea for you, as a <u>first</u> step, to

(A) interview the person who wrote the letter at his home
(B) speak to the people in your department who have knowledge of the matter complained about
(C) turn this over to one of your subordinates who is not very busy
(D) write the person a letter telling him that the matter he complains about is being looked into and will be settled to his satisfaction

78. A subordinate whom you supervise has an accident on the job and is hurt. In your written report of this accident to your own superior it is <u>least</u> important for you to include information about

(A) the subordinate's attitude toward other employees

(B) the tool used when the accident happened
(C) what you plan to do to prevent such accidents in the future
(D) when the accident happened

79. Just before the end of a new gardener's probationary period, his supervisor turned in a report to his superior on the new employee's work and record during the probationary period. In her report, the supervisor did not make any recommendation whether the new employee should be kept on after his probationary period. The supervisor's action was

(A) bad because it is the gardener's responsibility to make a recommendation whether the new employee should be kept on after the probationary period
(B) good because she should be impartial to all new employees
(C) bad because the new employee will not know if he is going to be kept on the job or not
(D) good because it is the job of "higher-ups" to decide if new employees should be kept on after the end of probation

80. Suppose that your supervisor has asked you to investigate a new gardening procedure, and give him a written report with a recommendation whether the new procedure should be used in the agency. It would probably be best for you to put your recommendation

(A) any place in the report where you can fit it in without too much trouble
(B) at the end of the report after you have given the facts of your investigation
(C) in the middle of the report
(D) on a separate attached sheet

## Answer Key

| | | | | |
|---|---|---|---|---|
| 1. D | 17. B | 33. D | 49. C | 65. C |
| 2. B | 18. C | 34. B | 50. A | 66. D |
| 3. A | 19. A | 35. A | 51. A | 67. A |
| 4. B | 20. D | 36. A | 52. D | 68. B |
| 5. B | 21. C | 37. C | 53. C | 69. C |
| 6. A | 22. C | 38. C | 54. A | 70. B |
| 7. D | 23. B | 39. B | 55. C | 71. D |
| 8. D | 24. A | 40. C | 56. B | 72. D |
| 9. C | 25. B | 41. A | 57. D | 73. C |
| 10. B | 26. A | 42. D | 58. B | 74. C |
| 11. B | 27. C | 43. D | 59. C | 75. D |
| 12. A | 28. D | 44. B | 60. A | 76. A |
| 13. C | 29. B | 45. B | 61. D | 77. B |
| 14. A | 30. E | 46. A | 62. B | 78. A |
| 15. C | 31. C | 47. A | 63. B | 79. A |
| 16. B | 32. A | 48. B | 64. A | 80. B |

# SAMPLE PRACTICE EXAMINATION III

DIRECTIONS FOR ANSWERING QUESTIONS

Each question has four suggested answers, lettered A,B,C, and D. Decide which one is the best answer, find the question number on the sample answer sheet, and darken the area with a soft pencil which corresponds to the answer that you have selected.

The time allowed for the entire examination is 3½ hours.

1. It is <u>not</u> an important function of phosphorus in the soil to help

    (A) good root development
    (B) make the soil alkaline
    (C) produce an abundance of fruits and seeds
    (D) the formation of strong cell walls

2. An element necessary for the nutrition of plants that is normally obtained from the soil, rather than from water or the atmosphere, is

    (A) carbon
    (B) hydrogen
    (C) oxygen
    (D) nitrogen

3. "Fresh manure should never be used where it will come in direct contact with the root formation of the plants." The most important reason for this is that the

    (A) manure is liable to cause severe burning
    (B) manure may drain the soil and dehydrate the roots
    (C) nitrogen content of the manure may have harmful effects
    (D) nutrient value of the manure has not yet reached its maximum

4. "Beginning to grow from a seed to a plant" is a description of

(A) cultivating
(B) germinating
(C) propagating
(D) transplanting

5. Which one of these is a deficiency disease in plants?

(A) black rot
(B) chlorosis
(C) leaf spot
(D) mildew

6. The best way of improving the structure of sandy soils is by

(A) autumn spading or plowing
(B) frequent watering
(C) the addition of large quantities of organic matter
(D) the use of inorganic fertilizers

7. In gardening, to "drill" seed means to

(A) pack it into the earth by rolling
(B) rake it into the soil
(C) scatter it by hand or machine
(D) sow it in rows

8. "Lime should never be used in combination with animal manures or with nitrogenous fertilizers." The most important reason for this is that it would cause

(A) lime-induced chlorosis
(B) the acidity of the soil to increase to a point unfavorable for plant growth
(C) the alkalinity of the soil to increase to a point unfavorable for plant growth
(D) the rapid release of ammonia

9. Which one of these materials will best increase the water holding capacity of the soil?

(A) bonemeal
(B) lime
(C) peat
(D) potash

10. The addition of humus to the soil does <u>not</u>

(A) increase its water holding capacity
(B) modify soil structure

(C) prevent leaching of soluble plant foods
(D) slow up bacterial action

11. An advantage of leaving grass clippings on the lawn is that it

(A) helps maintain the humus supply in the soil
(B) prevents the grass roots from becoming too wet
(C) protects the roots from the drying effects of wind and sun
(D) tends to make the soil more compact

12. Which one of the following is <u>least</u> important for satisfactory growth of lawn grasses?

(A) iron
(B) nitrogen
(C) phosphorus
(D) potash

13. Moss in a lawn is usually a sign of

(A) bad soil drainage
(B) low soil fertility
(C) poor soil texture
(D) soil acidity

14. The best time for sowing lawn grasses is usually the

(A) early autumn
(B) early spring
(C) late winter
(D) summer

15. Which one is <u>not</u> usually a cause of brown spots in a lawn?

(A) burning from unequal distribution of fertilizer
(B) excessive soil acidity
(C) fungus diseases
(D) unfavorable weather conditions

16. Which one of the following statements about crab-grass is <u>not</u> true?

(A) it is an annual
(B) it is killed by the first light frost
(C) its seed germinates in the fall
(D) it thrives in the full sun

17. A disadvantage of using rotted manure as a lawn fertilizer is that it

(A) increases the number of soil bacteria
(B) often brings weed seeds into the lawn
(C) often burns the roots of grass
(D) usually burns the blades of grass

18. A chemical which effectively controls crabgrass is

(A) chlordane
(B) corrosive sublimate
(C) dieldrin
(D) potassium cyanate

19. Kentucky bluegrass does <u>not</u>

(A) germinate more slowly than many other permanent lawn grasses
(B) prefer a cool climate
(C) require abundant moisture
(D) require a highly acid soil

20. The grass that must usually be established by means of stolons is

(A) creeping bent
(B) Kentucky bluegrass
(C) perennial ryegrass
(D) redtop

21. Lawns should be rolled lightly

(A) at least twice during the summer
(B) before the frost sets in
(C) during the winter
(D) not more than once or twice during the spring

22. Which one of these grasses is <u>least</u> suitable for use in a mixture for a dry, shady location?

(A) chewings fescue
(B) colonial bent
(C) Kentucky bluegrass
(D) redtop

23. When planting a new lawn, the best way to add lime to a highly acidic soil is

(A) in one application after growth has started

(B) in one application before seeding
(C) in several applications after growth has started
(D) in several applications before seeding

24. "Organic fertilizers that are to be applied to lawns should supply nitrogen from a number of sources." This recommendation should be followed mainly because it will

(A) avoid the chance of poor nutrition due to poor products if the nitrogen is supplied from only one source
(B) avoid the danger of delayed nitrogen burn since the nitrogen will be released over a period of time
(C) make it possible to apply the fertilizer at any time of the year
(D) make the soil neutral

25. A characteristic of bent grasses is that they

(A) are less subject to attacks from fungus diseases than most other lawn grasses
(B) are not tolerant of soil acidity
(C) can stand close mowing
(D) do well on dry soils

Each of questions 26 to 30 gives the botanical or scientific name of a common plant. For each one, select the correct common name from Column I.

| | Column I |
|---|---|
| 26. ilex | (A) firethorn |
| 27. ligustrum | (B) holly |
| 28. lonicera | (C) honeysuckle |
| 29. pyracantha | (D) lilac |
| 30. syringa | (E) privet |

31. The chief purpose for "heeling-in" of shrubs is to

(A) improve their form
(B) keep their roots from drying out
(C) prevent the invasion of weeds
(D) promote their natural increase in number

32. Of the following, the best time for transplanting deciduous trees and shrubs is generally

(A) early spring
(B) early summer
(C) late summer
(D) mid-winter

33. Which best describes foliar feeding?

(A) leaves getting food from the rest of the plant
(B) leaves making food for the rest of the plant
(C) leaves taking in food for the rest of the plant
(D) roots taking in food for the rest of the plant

34. Which one of these shrubs has a preference for lime?

(A) azalea
(B) firethorn
(C) pieris (floribunda)
(D) rhododendron

35. Which one of the following groups of shrubs is most likely to provide blooms throughout the spring?

(A) catawba rhododendron, sweet pepperbush, swamp rose
(B) hydrangea, rose of sharon, golden bells
(C) witch hazel (hamamelis), flowering quince, golden bells
(D) witch hazel (hamamelis), rose of sharon, catawba rhododendron

36. Which one of these is an evergreen shrub?

(A) cornus paniculata (gray dogwood)
(B) rhododendron catawbiense
(C) spiraea thunbergi
(D) viburnum tomentosum

37. Which one of the following is best to put in the bottom of a hole dug for planting a bare-rooted tree?

(A) complete fertilizer
(B) fresh manure
(C) lime
(D) topsoil

38. Which one of these will grow best in a wet location?

(A) japanese barberry (berberis thunbergi)
(B) rugosa rose
(C) sweet pepper bush (clethra alnifolia)
(D) wayfaring tree (viburnum lantana)

39. Pruning is <u>not</u> usually done in order to

(A) control the structure of a tree or shrub
(B) improve the appearance of a plant
(C) increase the height to which a plant grows
(D) increase the quantity and quality of flowers and fruit

40. For most evergreen hedges, the best season of the year for clipping is

(A) spring
(B) summer
(C) autumn
(D) winter

Each of questions 41 to 45 gives the name of a bulb, corm, or tuber which may be classified under one of the headings in Column II. For each one, select the heading from Column II under which it is most correctly classified.

| | Column II |
|---|---|
| 41. begonia | (A) spring flowering |
| 42. caladium | (B) summer flowering |
| 43. colchicum | (C) autumn flowering |
| 44. hyacinth | |
| 45. narcissus | |

46. Which one is most likely to be needed by perennials during periods when there is a great deal of rain?

(A) calcium
(B) ground limestone
(C) sulphate of ammonia
(D) super phosphate

47. "Pinching back" is the

(A) nipping out of a terminal bud of a plant to help the plant become bushy
(B) pruning of leaves that have shrivelled from an early frost
(C) removal of leaves of a plant close to the main stem
(D) shrivelling of the leaf tips of a plant from fungus infection

48. Clumps of some perennials must be divided after a few years in order for them to continue to thrive. A perennial that should be lifted and divided <u>every</u>

year is

(A) chrysanthemum
(B) hardy aster
(C) peony
(D) phlox

49. A good fertilizer should be applied to perennials twice a year. The best time to make this application is in

(A) early spring before active growth and in late summer
(B) early summer and in the fall
(C) spring after active growth and in early summer
(D) spring after active growth and in late summer

Each of questions 50 to 53 gives the name of a plant that may be classified under one of the descriptions of color of blooms in Column III. For each plant, select the description from Column III that best describes the usual color of bloom.

| | Column III |
|---|---|
| 50. cockscomb | (A) blue or pink |
| 51. forget-me-not | (B) greenish-yellow |
| 52. mignonette | (C) white |
| 53. sweet alyssum | (D) yellow to crimson |

54. Of the following annuals, the one that best tolerates poor quality soil is

(A) gypsophila
(B) petunia
(C) rocket larkspur
(D) zinnia

55. The one of the following plants that is a biennial is

(A) candytuft
(B) canterbury bells
(C) marigold
(D) snapdragon

56. The one of the following plants that is most suitable as a ground cover is

(A) creeping charlie

(B) ground ivy
(C) japanese honeysuckle
(D) japanese pachysandra

57. Of the following plants used for ground cover, the one that is evergreen is

(A) candytuft (iberis sempervirens)
(B) forget-me-nots (mysotis palustris semperflorens)
(C) lemon thyme (thymus citriodorus)
(D) wall pepper (sedum acre)

58. "Hedges under trees are usually unsatisfactory." The chief reason for this is that

(A) diseased trees may result in diseased hedges
(B) the landscape becomes too monotonous
(C) the tree roots are competing with the hedges for nourishment
(D) trimming the hedge becomes more difficult

59. The one of the following plants that generally requires more than one trimming a year when used as a hedge is

(A) arborvitae
(B) hemlock
(C) privet
(D) yew

60. Of the following, the main advantage in using euonymus slatus (winged burningbush) as a hedge is that it

(A) grows best in shade
(B) grows to a maximum height of 3 ft.
(C) produces bright-red flowers in July and August
(D) requires no clipping

61. Of the following, the best shape for a formal, clipped hedge is

(A) taller than it is wide
(B) wider at the bottom than at the top
(C) wider at the top than at the bottom
(D) wider than it is tall

Each of questions 62 to 65 gives the name of a shrub which may be classified under one of the heights of growth in Column IV. For each shrub, select the height in Column IV which best describes its normal height of growth.

| | Column IV |
|---|---|
| 62. beauty bush (Kolkwitzia amabilis) | (A) 1½ to 3 ft. |
| 63. garden lilac (Syringa vulgaris) | (B) 4 to 8 ft. |
| 64. mountain andromeda (Pieris floribunda) | (C) 8 to 15 ft. |
| 65. vanhoutte spiraea (Spiraea Vanhouttei) | |

66. Dieldrin is a chemical used most frequently

(A) as a dormant spray in early spring
(B) as a fungicide
(C) to arrest spore production
(D) to grub-proof lawns

67. Snow mold is a type of

(A) coldframe used during winter snow
(B) fungus disease
(C) soil rich in humus
(D) winter grass

Each of questions 68 to 73 gives the name of a chemical compound used in gardening that may be classified under one of the headings in Column V. For each chemical compound, select the heading from Column V under which it is most correctly classified.

| | Column V |
|---|---|
| 68. Acti-Dione | (A) antibiotic |
| 69. captan | (B) organic fungicide |
| 70. carolate | (C) systemic fungicide |
| 71. Demetron | (D) systemic insecticide |
| 72. fermate | |
| 73. sodium selenate | |

74. In gardening, arsenate of lead is most commonly used as a

(A) contact insecticide
(B) fungicide
(C) soil conditioner
(D) stomach poison

Each of questions 75 to 80 gives the name of an insect that may be classified under one of the headings in Column VI. For each insect, select the heading from Column VI under which it is most correctly classified.

Column VI

(A) insect with chewing mouth parts
(B) insect with sucking mouth parts

75. aphid
76. beetle
77. caterpillar
78. grasshopper
79. leaf-hopper
80. scale

81. When used in pruning, the pruning saw with teeth on both edges is

    (A) best for removing large limbs
    (B) best for removing small limbs
    (C) likely to cause injury to the worker, no matter how careful he is
    (D) likely to wound the tree when used in close quarters

82. Of the following statements about the standard steel rake, the one that is most correct is that it is

    (A) easier to use than any other rake
    (B) suitable for all raking duties
    (C) the least expensive rake on the market
    (D) used particularly for working the soil

83. When used for weeding, the common garden hoe should be handled as a

    (A) chopping or slicing tool
    (B) digging tool
    (C) drawing tool
    (D) pushing and pulling tool

84. When gathering leaves and twigs, the large wooden rake should be used with

    (A) brush strokes, like a broom
    (B) long sliding strokes, the teeth being lifted only to clear the debris
    (C) push and pull strokes, avoiding tearing the sod
    (D) pushing strokes in two directions, at right angles, over the whole planted area

85. Thoroughly coating the inside of the galvanized iron tank of a hand sprayer with black asphaltum will

(A) add elements beneficial to plant life to the contents of the sprayer
(B) increase the efficiency of the sprayer
(C) lengthen the life of the tank
(D) purify the water going through the tank

86. If a garden tool becomes very dull, a new edge is best developed by using

(A) a carborundum wheel
(B) a file
(C) an oilstone
(D) a whetstone

87. A pointed tool used to make holes in soft ground for planting bulbs or setting small plants is known as a

(A) dibble
(B) hand cultivator
(C) spiker
(D) spud

88. The main reason why pruning shears should be kept sharp is to prevent

(A) extra tension between blade cutting edges
(B) rust from forming on the blades
(C) the user's hand from being pinched
(D) unnecessary damage to the plant when pruning

89. Of the following, the tool that is most useful in firming newly laid sod is the

(A) half-moon edger
(B) sod beater
(C) sod-cutting iron
(D) spading fork

90. Before storing a power lawn mower at the end of the season, it is wise to

(A) drain the crankcase and fill with fresh oil
(B) fill the gasoline tank
(C) remove the air filter
(D) rinse the oil filter in gasoline, but leave the oil in

91. Suppose that you are appointed as a gardener. You find that some of the tools need either repair or replacement. You should

(A) delay the operations requiring the use of these tools and work only on other jobs until your supervisor becomes aware of the situation
(B) report the condition of your tools to your supervisor immediately
(C) wait until you are sure of your job before you complain about any conditions of work
(D) work with the equipment you have as best you can and wait until the end of the budget year to report your equipment needs

92. Suppose you notice that two of your assistants get into arguments whenever they work together on a job. You should first

(A) find out what is causing the arguments between them
(B) recommend that one of them be transferred from your supervision
(C) report the situation to your supervisor
(D) warn both that if this happens again you will have to take severe disciplinary action

93. In a report requesting replacement of inadequate gardening tools, it would be <u>least</u> important to include.

(A) a recommendation as to the types of tools to be purchased
(B) the reason why the tools cannot be used any longer
(C) the titles of employees who will be using these tools
(D) the types of tools needing replacement

94. Suppose that an employee falls off a truck and suffers a head injury. You should

(A) give her first aid and call a doctor
(B) immediately call a taxi and send her home
(C) send her to the borough office for examination
(D) send her to the nearest police precinct to report the accident and for first aid treatment

95. Suppose that a temporary assistant is assigned to you to help with a particular summer project in

one of the city parks. The first day on the job he returns from his lunch hour one-half hour late. You should

(A) dismiss the employee since there is no point in training an obviously poor worker
(B) explain the rules of the department to him and warn him not to repeat this action
(C) overlook the action since this is only a temporary worker
(D) suspend the employee for the day with proper salary deduction

96. If you find that two of your assistants tend to be careless in the use of tools, you should

(A) ask that they be transferred
(B) call each one aside and talk to them privately
(C) call the workers together at a meeting to discuss the problem
(D) personally issue all tools yourself

97. As gardener, you are assigned to be in charge of a number of temporary workers who are to report to you the following day for a special assignment. You find that you cannot be present that day because of urgent personal business. You should

(A) assign an experienced assistant to substitute for you
(B) contact the temporary workers and advise them to report the day after
(C) leave written instructions for the workers as to how to proceed with the job
(D) report the facts to your supervisor and await further instructions

98. Of the following, the best way for a gardener to get the cooperation of his subordinates is to

(A) set low standards of work performance
(B) be informal and make friends with his workers
(C) be fair and cooperative himself
(D) be easy going in applying department rules and regulations

99. Of the following, the most important reason for a gardener to regularly check the work of the employees under her is to

(A) be able to give them a service rating at the end of the year

(B) increase their output
(C) let them see that she is interested in their progress
(D) make sure that the work is being performed satisfactorily

100. When assigning work to subordinates, a gardener should

(A) be sure to give the same amount of work to each
(B) consider each employee's individual ability and special skills
(C) give the most work to the employee who usually shirks his responsibilities
(D) give the simple jobs to those who have been in the department the longest

## Answer Key

| | | | | |
|---|---|---|---|---|
| 1. B | 21. D | 41. B | 61. B | 81. D |
| 2. D | 22. C | 42. B | 62. B | 82. B |
| 3. A | 23. D | 43. C | 63. C | 83. A |
| 4. B | 24. B | 44. A | 64. A | 84. B |
| 5. B | 25. C | 45. A | 65. B | 85. C |
| 6. C | 26. B | 46. C | 66. D | 86. A |
| 7. D | 27. E | 47. A | 67. B | 87. A |
| 8. D | 28. C | 48. B | 68. A | 88. D |
| 9. C | 29. A | 49. C | 69. B | 89. B |
| 10. D | 30. D | 50. D | 70. C | 90. A |
| 11. A | 31. B | 51. A | 71. D | 91. B |
| 12. A | 32. A | 52. B | 72. B | 92. A |
| 13. B | 33. C | 53. C | 73. D | 93. C |
| 14. A | 34. B | 54. B | 74. D | 94. A |
| 15. B | 35. C | 55. B | 75. B | 95. B |
| 16. C | 36. B | 56. D | 76. A | 96. C |
| 17. B | 37. D | 57. A | 77. A | 97. D |
| 18. D | 38. C | 58. C | 78. A | 98. C |
| 19. D | 39. C | 59. C | 79. B | 99. D |
| 20. A | 40. A | 60. D | 80. B | 100. B |

# SAMPLE PRACTICE EXAMINATION IV

DIRECTIONS FOR ANSWERING QUESTIONS

Each question has four suggested answers, lettered A, B, C, and D. Decide which one is the best answer, find the question number on the sample answer sheet, and darken the area with a soft pencil which corresponds to the answer that you have selected. Then test yourself again. If you show improvement, you may congratulate yourself on having picked up a few more points on the actual exam.

The time allowed for the entire examination is 3½ hours.

1. In gardening, the main purpose of establishing good drainage in a planted area is to

    (A) confine the available water to the root area of plants
    (B) prevent the loss of needed moisture
    (C) provide additional moisture to growing plants
    (D) remove excess water from the planted area

2. A disadvantage of the use of fresh barnyard manure for soil amendment is that such manure

    (A) has little plant food value
    (B) has many weed seeds
    (C) makes the soil too acid
    (D) makes the soil too wet

3. Peat moss is <u>least</u> valuable when used as a

    (A) plant food
    (B) rooting medium

(C) soil conditioner
(D) winter cover on the ground around the base of plants

4. The addition of organic matter to the soil is often recommended. Of the following, the one that is <u>not</u> classed as organic matter is

(A) leaf mold
(B) lime
(C) manure
(D) peat moss

5. The effect of lime when added to the soil is to

(A) give the soil a finer texture
(B) make the soil more acidic
(C) make the soil more alkaline
(D) provide plant food directly to the plants

6. Of the following, the most accurate statement about humus is that it

(A) consists of decomposed animal and vegetable matter
(B) has no plant food value
(C) holds moisture poorly
(D) is the mineral part of the soil

7. "Clay soils should not be cultivated when they are wet." Of the following, the most important reason for this rule is that

(A) clay soils cannot be spaded when wet
(B) excessive soil moisture will be lost by evaporation
(C) moisture remaining on tools will cause them to rust
(D) the soil will dry into a hard solid mass

8. To "force" plants means to cause them to grow

(A) beyond their normal life cycle
(B) earlier and more quickly than normally by providing them with unnaturally stimulating or favorable conditions
(C) in a certain form or shape with the aid of physical supports and by pinching off all side growth
(D) in an otherwise infertile soil by limiting the number of plants to be grown in a given area

9. To say that a seed has "germinated" means that it has

(A) become infected with a harmful plant disease
(B) begun to grow into a plant
(C) developed abnormally
(D) rotted because of too much moisture

10. The term "hardy" is usually applied to a plant which can

(A) be transplanted easily
(B) go without water for a considerable period of time
(C) live from year to year
(D) withstand cold

11. In gardening, to "broadcast" seed means to

(A) rake it into the soil
(B) scatter it by hand
(C) sow it in rows
(D) test it for purity

12. The term "green manure" usually refers to

(A) a crop grown to be plowed under in order to improve the soil
(B) a freshly produced animal manure
(C) a manure manufactured artificially out of chemicals
(D) the material obtained from a compost pile

13. To "mulch" means to

(A) allow a prepared seed bed to stay idle for several days before planting
(B) cover the ground around plants with light litter such as leaves or straw
(C) encourage excessive growth of plants by overfeeding
(D) remove unwanted growth from plants

14. A fertilizer that is readily "soluble"

(A) becomes available to plants for food very quickly after application
(B) becomes "fixed" and held in the soil when applied

(C) is not likely to be washed out of the soil in the drainage water and may be applied in large doses
(D) must be dissolved before application.

15. Furnishing plants with an excessive amount of nitrogen results in

(A) abundant flower and fruit production but retarded stem and foilage growth
(B) increased foliage, flower and fruit growth
(C) increased root growth but reduced stem and foliage growth
(D) luxuriant stem and foliage growth at the expense of flower and fruit production

16. Of the following, a major purpose of the coldframe is to

(A) keep plants cold before transplanting
(B) protect growing plants by supplying artificial heat
(C) protect plants from burning by excessive sunlight
(D) start seedlings in advance of the outdoor season

17. Of the following hand tools used in the garden, the one largest in overall size is the

(A) dibble
(B) spading fork
(C) trowel
(D) hoe

18. Annuals are plants that

(A) complete their life cycle in one year and then die
(B) flower every year
(C) live from year to year
(D) produce seed the second year of growth

19. The dusting of plants to control insects and diseases is

(A) frequently done with materials that are also used as sprays
(B) more effective than the spraying of plants for the same purpose

(C) not recommended because of injury to the worker from inhalation of the dust
(D) recommended only where the underside of the leaves cannot be reached by a spray

20. The best time to sow lawn grass seed is usually in

(A) early summer
(B) mid-summer
(C) the fall
(D) the spring

21. If ground that has been newly prepared for a lawn must remain idle for several days before seed is sown, it is desirable to rake the surface from time to time during this period with a steel garden rake. Of the following, the most important purpose of this raking is usually to

(A) destroy weed seedlings as they start to grow
(B) fill in depressions
(C) insure even distribution of fertilizer that has been applied
(D) level off high spots

22. In the planting and care of a new lawn it is <u>not</u> considered good practice to

(A) give the ground a light rolling after the seed has been sown and top-dressed
(B) rake the soil just before the seed is sown
(C) sow half the seed while walking back and forth in one direction and the other half while walking back and forth at right angles over the same area
(D) water heavily till the seed germinates, then to water lightly

23. In permanent lawn seed mixtures, the "nurse" grasses often included because they come up quickly and offer protection to the slower growing permanent grasses are

(A) fescues and redtop
(B) Kentucky blue and fescues
(C) Kentucky blue and rye
(D) rye and redtop

24. The type of clover most commonly used in lawn seed mixtures is

(A) alsike clover
(B) crimson clover
(C) red clover
(D) white clover

25. It is most correct to state that crab grass is usually

    (A) considered to be a lawn weed
    (B) included in lawn seed mixtures because it is quick to grow
    (C) nitrogen fixing
    (D) tall growing

26. It is most correct to state that the dandelion

    (A) has short, fine roots
    (B) is considered a lawn weed
    (C) is distinguished by its large white flowers
    (D) will die when its top is cut

27. A properly shaped formal hedge should be

    (A) flat at the top
    (B) narrower at the bottom than at the top
    (C) narrower at the top than at the bottom
    (D) of the same width, top and bottom

28. When privet hedges are planted, they are often cut back to within a few inches of the ground. The main purpose of this is usually to

    (A) insure dense growth from the ground up
    (B) remove diseased or dead members
    (C) remove interfering branches
    (D) speed up root development

29. Privet hedges are most commonly propagated by

    (A) budding
    (B) dividing the stem of the parent plant
    (C) grafting
    (D) rooting cuttings in moist earth

30. Of the following, the best way to store nursery stock that cannot be planted for a few days is to

    (A) keep it in a tub of water
    (B) lay it flat on the ground in an exposed sunny location where it may receive the benefit of adequate light and air
    (C) lay the root end in a trench dug in the earth and cover with soil
    (D) unwrap it and put it in a dark, dry location

31. Of the following, the <u>least</u> important reason for cultivating the ground around a shrub border is to

    (A) aerate the ground
    (B) break the crust that forms where wet soil dries
    (C) destroy surface roots
    (D) kill weeds

Each of the questions 32 to 40 gives the name of a plant that may be classified under one of the headings given in column I. Write the capital letter preceding the group under which each plant is most correctly classified.

| | Column I |
|---|---|
| 32. azalea | (A) narrow-leaved evergreen |
| 33. dogwood | (B) broad-leaved evergreen |
| 34. forsythia | (C) deciduous tree |
| 35. ginkgo | (D) deciduous shrub |
| 36. juniper | |
| 37. mountain laurel | |
| 38. rhododendron | |
| 39. spiraea | |
| 40. spruce | |

Each of the questions 41 to 46 gives the name of a bulb, corn, or tuber. For each one, write the letter A if it should be planted outdoors in the spring, the letter B if it should be planted outdoors in the fall

| | Column I |
|---|---|
| 41. dahlia | (A) should be planted outdoors in the spring |
| 42. gladiolus | (B) should be planted outdoors in the fall |
| 43. hardy lily | |
| 44. hyacinth | |
| 45. narcissus | |
| 46. tulip | |

47. When planting and growing bulbs, a good procedure to follow is to

    (A) allow a space about twice the diameter of a bulb between one bulb and the next
    (B) plant all bulbs at least 4 in. below the surface of the ground, regardless of size
    (C) plant spring flowering bulbs in November and December to prevent root formation in the fall
    (D) plant summer flowering bulbs the previous fall

48. When growing bulbs and corms it is good practice to

(A) cut all foliage close to the ground shortly after the flowers have formed
(B) leave the bulbs or corms in the ground until the foliage has completely matured and withered
(C) leave all bulbs or corms undisturbed in the ground from year to year
(D) lift the bulbs or corms from the ground as soon as the flowers have withered

49. Of the following, the country from which the most bulbs are imported into the United States is

(A) Denmark
(B) France
(C) Germany
(D) Holland

50. In the growth and culture of gladiolus corms it is most correct to state that

(A) corms measuring less than 2 in. in diameter will not give good blooms
(B) small cormels are formed under the base of the old corm when the new corm fails to mature fully
(C) the larger the root plate or basal area from which the roots arise, the younger the corm
(D) the planted corm withers up during the growing period and a new one forms on top of it

51. The one of the following <u>least</u> suitable for use as a ground cover is

(A) english ivy
(B) japanese pachysandra
(C) periwinkle
(D) zinnia

52. Pinching off the top of a growing annual will usually

(A) induce a tall, lanky growth
(B) kill the plant
(C) make the plant branch
(D) stop further growth

53. The one of the following that cannot usually be accomplished by pruning of a plant is

(A) an improvement in its form
(B) an increase in its flower production

(C) an increase in its structural strength
(D) a permanent change in its natural growing habit

54. The pruning of early spring flowering shrubs is best done

(A) a week or two after the flowers have fallen
(B) in late summer
(C) just before growth starts in the spring
(D) while the shrubs are dormant

55. The most accurate of the following statements about the japanese beetle is that

(A) it is a chewing insect and can be controlled by the use of a stomach poison
(B) it is injurious in its adult stage but harmless as a grub
(C) it will attack the flowers but not the leaves of plants
(D) the period of greatest feeding activity of the adult beetle in the New York City area occurs during June and July

56. Aphids, garden insects popularly called plant lice,

(A) are beneficial because they eat other harmful insects
(B) are best controlled by using a stomach poison
(C) eat the leaves of plants
(D) feed by sucking the sap from plants

57. Of the following insects, the one <u>not</u> generally considered beneficial is the

(A) bee
(B) ladybird beetle
(C) praying mantis
(D) red spider

58. A 5-10-5 fertilizer contains approximately

(A) 5% nitrogen
(B) 10% nitrogen
(C) 20% nitrogen
(D) 25% nitrogen

59. Of the following, the most accurate statement about fertilizers is that

(A) an organic fertilizer should be wetted down as soon as it is applied

(B) commercial or chemical fertilizers must be applied in heavy concentrations because of their low plant food content
(C) some fertilizers consist of a combination of organic and inorganic materials
(D) the plant food in an organic fertilizer becomes available to plants more quickly than the plant food in an inorganic fertilizer

60. A "complete" fertilizer is one which contains

(A) nitrogen, phosphorus and potassium
(B) nitrogen, phosphorus and sodium
(C) nitrogen, potassium and calcium
(D) nitrogen, potassium and iron

61. Late summer application of nitrogenous fertilizer to woody plants is inadvisable mainly because

(A) frost-sensitive tender new growth is encouraged
(B) nitrogenous fertilizer is not the best fertilizer for woody plants
(C) the fertilizer will be leached away by spring thaw and rains before it can be used by the plants next summer
(D) there is insufficient rainfall at this time

62. The one of the following that supplies mainly phosphorus to plants is

(A) bonemeal
(B) dried blood
(C) nitrate of soda
(D) wood ashes

63. In the New York City area the average frost free date in the spring comes during the

(A) first half of March
(B) second half of March
(C) first half of April
(D) second half of April

64. In the New York City area the average first killing frost in the fall comes during the

(A) first half of October
(B) second half of October
(C) first half of November
(D) second half of November

65. The Long Island Agricultural and Technical Institute is located at

(A) Farmingdale
(B) Garden City
(C) Hempstead
(D) Mineola

66. The New York State College of Agriculture is located at

(A) Albany
(B) Ithaca
(C) Syracuse
(D) Utica

67. The practice of hilling or earthing-up soil around the roots of shrubs and hedges during the growing season is generally

(A) desirable mainly because it prevents sun scorch
(B) desirable mainly because it roots the plants more firmly
(C) undesirable mainly because it detracts from the appearance of normally attractive looking plants
(D) undesirable mainly because it develops a shallow root system readily injured in a period of drought

68. When propagating plants by means of cuttings, the cuttings should

(A) be permanently planted as soon as they are removed from the parent plant
(B) be planted outdoors when they have developed sufficient root growth
(C) have all the leaves removed before they are placed in the rooting medium
(D) have foliage to the base of the stem when inserted in the rooting medium

69. Conifers are

(A) bulbous plants
(B) flower bearing shrubs
(C) trees bearing fruit
(D) trees bearing woody cones

70. The <u>least</u> accurate of the following statements about the plane tree is that it

(A) has a dense maple-like foliage
(B) has a tough bark that is difficult to remove
(C) is also known as the buttonball tree
(D) is frequently used for street planting

71. In the trunk of a tree, the

(A) cambium is the growing portion of the trunk
(B) heartwood is located next to the outer bark
(C) sap flows down in the sapwood and up in the heartwood
(D) sap flows up and down in the innermost portion of the trunk

72. When spaded into a neutral soil, oak leafmold will generally tend to

(A) make the soil acid
(B) make the soil alkaline
(C) make the soil more neutral
(D) have no effect on the acidity or alkalinity of the soil

73. The most accurate of the following statements is that arborvitae is

(A) a broad-leaved evergreen
(B) an extremely rapid grower and requires very frequent clipping
(C) suitable for use as hedge material
(D) the botanical name for the genus commonly called thuja

74. A neutral soil is indicated by a pH reading of

(A) 1
(B) 7
(C) 14
(D) 20

75. An alkaline soil is indicated if upon contact with the soil

(A) blue litmus paper turns purple
(B) blue litmus paper turns white
(C) red litmus paper turns blue
(D) red litmus paper turns green

76. The one of the following that is <u>least</u> suitable for use as formal hedge material is

(A) abelia
(B) California privet
(C) japanese barberry
(D) yew

77. In gardening, a "herbaceous" plant

(A) dies to the ground
(B) is perennial
(C) produces a flower
(D) produces a fruit

78. In pruning, when a part of a twig or branch is cut off, the cut should be made

(A) about one quarter of an inch above a bud
(B) halfway between two buds
(C) immediately above and as close to a bud as possible
(D) just below a bud

79. It is most correct to state that in the control of insect pests of plants

(A) contact insecticides are most often used against insects with biting and chewing mouth parts
(B) copper compounds are most often used as contact insecticides
(C) lead arsenate is most often used as a stomach poison
(D) stomach poisons are most often used against insects with piercing and sucking mouth parts

80. Insecticides and fungicides that are "incompatible"

(A) are useless unless applied as a mixture
(B) have a lasting effect
(C) must be applied in liquid solution
(D) will injure the plant if applied in combination

81. The one of the following recommended for use against broad-leaved weeds in a lawn is

(A) chlordane
(B) DDT
(C) potassium cyanate
(D) 2,4-D

82. Brown patch is a disease of grasses caused by

(A) fungus
(B) an insect
(C) excessive alkalinity
(D) insufficient moisture

83. Bordeaux mixture is most properly used as

    (A) a fertilizer
    (B) a fungicide
    (C) an insecticide
    (D) a soil conditioner

84. With regard to oil sprays, it is most correct to state that they are

    (A) best applied during the summer months when insects are actively feeding
    (B) best sprayed on the plant without diluting the oil with water
    (C) injurious to plant life and should not be used
    (D) used chiefly for spraying plants in a dormant condition

85. Materials used to kill fungi that cause plant diseases usually consist of some form of

    (A) arsenic
    (B) lead
    (C) sulphur
    (D) zinc

86. Of the following flowering shrubs, the one that flowers latest is

    (A) almond
    (B) althea (rose of sharon)
    (C) lonicera fragrantissima (bush honeysuckle)
    (D) spiraea vanhouttei (bridal wreath)

87. Of the following flowering shrubs, the one that flowers earliest is

    (A) buddleia (butterfly-bush)
    (B) common lilac
    (C) hydrangea
    (D) weigela

88. The one of the following that is an annual is

    (A) columbine
    (B) cosmos
    (C) english daisy
    (D) lily-of-the-valley

89. Written instructions are left by your supervisor (who will be absent from work for two days) to perform a task you feel is completely unnecessary. You should

(A) hold off performing the task until your supervisor returns
(B) perform the task despite your feelings
(C) convey your thoughts to your supervisor's superior
(D) consult with the other gardeners to see if they also have your opinion on the matter

90. If you are advised by your supervisor that work you are performing must be finished by a certain time, and if you find after performing a portion of it that it will not be possible to finish the work on time, you should

(A) work as fast as you can and do as much of the work that you can before the deadline
(B) request your fellow workers to help you get the job done on time
(C) finish those parts of the work during the time period which you think are most important
(D) immediately advise your boss that you will be unable to complete the job on time

## Answer Key

| | | | | |
|---|---|---|---|---|
| 1. D | 19. A | 37. B | 55. A | 73. C |
| 2. B | 20. C | 38. B | 56. D | 74. B |
| 3. A | 21. A | 39. D | 57. D | 75. C |
| 4. B | 22. D | 40. A | 58. A | 76. A |
| 5. C | 23. D | 41. A | 59. C | 77. A |
| 6. A | 24. D | 42. A | 60. A | 78. A |
| 7. D | 25. A | 43. B | 61. A | 79. C |
| 8. B | 26. B | 44. B | 62. A | 80. D |
| 9. B | 27. C | 45. B | 63. C | 81. D |
| 10. D | 28. A | 46. B | 64. C | 82. A |
| 11. B | 29. D | 47. A | 65. A | 83. B |
| 12. A | 30. C | 48. B | 66. B | 84. D |
| 13. B | 31. C | 49. D | 67. D | 85. C |
| 14. A | 32. B | 50. D | 68. B | 86. B |
| 15. D | 33. C | 51. D | 69. D | 87. B |
| 16. D | 34. D | 52. C | 70. B | 88. B |
| 17. B | 35. C | 53. D | 71. A | 89. B |
| 18. A | 36. A | 54. A | 72. A | 90. D |

# SAMPLE PRACTICE EXAMINATION V

DIRECTIONS FOR ANSWERING QUESTIONS

Answer all questions. Each question consists of a statement. You are to decide whether the statement is true or false. Mark the letter "T" if the statement is true or correct; mark the letter "F" if the statement is false or wrong.

The time allowed for the entire examination is 3 hours.

1. A bed of leaves or straw on the surface of the ground around plants helps to prevent loss of moisture from the soil.

2. An evergreen tree does not shed its leaves each year.

3. All insects are harmful to plant life.

4. Hedges should never be used as a border around walks and other landscaped areas.

5. When hedges are pruned it is considered good practice to cut them wider at the top than at the bottom in order to allow light to reach the bottom branches.

6. Leaves mixed with the soil will in time rot and add plant food to the soil

7. The usual reason why a tree guard is placed around a young tree is to protect the tree from possible injury.

8. During periods of hot weather it is desirable to give lawns a light watering.

9. The fall is usually the best time to sow lawn grass seed.

10. If a plant loses its leaves every fall it shows that the plant has not been planted properly.

11. Sandy soils drain quickly and dry rapidly.

12. Animal manures added to the soil improve its condition.

13. It is often hard to grow grass under a tree because the roots of the tree take away most of the water and plant food from the grass.

14. Any rust found on garden tools during the summer should be removed the following spring.

15. A gardener should know the tool best suited for each type of work so that the work will be made easier.

16. After use in gardening, tools should be stored in a cellar or basement because the dampness there is good for the metal parts.

17. As a help in keeping a good edge on tools, earth and grass clippings should be removed from the tools immediately after they are used.

18. A four-pronged spading fork is a good tool for digging up a garden area.

19. Chemicals used to kill plant insects usually can be applied only in a dissolved liquid form.

20. If a growing plant is to be moved from one spot to another it is good practice to first dig the new hole before digging up the plant that is to be moved in order to lessen the drying out of the roots.

21. Rapidly running water from an unattended hose can cause soil to wash off sloping planted areas.

22. A gardener who often comes late to work should expect his superiors to pay no attention to this lateness if his work is excellent.

23. It is all right for a gardener to give members of the public parts of plants growing in city parks provided he cuts off the parts carefully.

24. A gardener at work who sees a person throwing rubbish on the ground in a park should pay no attention since this is a matter for the Sanitation Department.

25. If your superior gives you an assignment you do not like, you should try to do a good job anyway.

26. If you know in advance that you will not be able

to report for work the next Thursday you should tell your superior immediately rather than wait to telephone him on the day of your absence.

Your answers to questions 27 to 29 must be based only on the information given in the following paragraph and not upon any other information you may have.

"It has long been customary to wrap damp sphagnum moss, peat moss or wood shavings around the roots and crowns of plants to prevent loss of moisture from living tissues during storage or in transit. The use of these materials has two major disadvantages. They make heavy, bulky packages which adds to the cost in mail-order shipping. In the case of dormant stock, if the moisture content of the packing is too high the plants may prematurely start new growth."

27. Usually sphagnum moss is wrapped around the roots and crown of plants to prevent loss of moisture during storage or in transit.

28. A cost factor in mail-order shipping is the bulkiness of the package.

29. Plants cannot start new growth if the moisture content of the packing is too high.

Your answers to questions 30 to 35 must be based only on the information given in the following paragraph and not upon any other information you may have.

"Lawn mowers as well as lawns suffer when the grass is cut too short. There is much more dust and dirt on the base of the blades of grass than higher up. This grit wears away the blades and the strike bar and quickly dulls them. Other bad practices are leaving the mower out overnight and failing to wipe the cutting edges dry after each mowing. A couple of dewy nights, a session with wet grass, and the sharp edge has rusted. The simple measure of wiping an oily rag across the edges of the blades and the cutting bar prevents rusting of these important surfaces."

30. When the grass is cut too short the lawn mower suffers.

31. There is more dirt on the base of a blade of grass than higher up.

32. The blades and the strike bar of a lawn mower are sharpened by the grit of the soil.

33. It is bad practice to leave the mower out overnight.

34. After each mowing the cutting edges of a mower should be wiped dry.

35. Wiping the edges of the blades and the cutting bar with an oily rag will not prevent rusting.

Your answers to questions 36 to 42 must be based only on the information given in the following paragraph and not upon any other information you may have.

"Many organic fertilizers can be used not only to add nutrients to the soil, but also to help build up humus content and thus increase its water holding capacity. Organic fertilizers are those derived entirely from animal or vegetable sources, whereas inorganic kinds are chemical. The most readily available complete organic fertilizers are the manures, and these alone do not contain enough nutrients to satisfy a garden for a whole season. Application of one or more kinds of manure to the soil is excellent in the spring and again in the fall."

36. Organic fertilizers can be used to help build up the humus content of the soil.

37. Nutrients cannot be added to the soil through the use of organic fertilizers.

38. Inorganic fertilizers are chemical ones.

39. The organic fertilizers are derived from vegetable or animal sources.

40. The manures are the most readily available complete organic fertilizer.

41. The manures contain enough nutrients to satisfy a garden for a whole season.

42. Application of manure to the soil is excellent in the spring and in the fall.

Your answers to questions 43 to 55 must be based only on the information given in the following paragraph and not upon any other information you may have.

"If roses are to bloom well they should not be neglected. Of the several measures to be taken, watering is one of the most important. A weekly soil soaking is recommended. Moisture should go down to the roots of the plants, where it is vitally needed, to a depth of about six inches. Taking the nozzle off the hose and letting water trickle into the soil is one way to do this."

"A four-inch layer of mulch on the surface of the soil will protect the roots of the rose plants against heat, cold and draught. Suitable mulches for roses include partly rotted stable manure, peat moss, compost, and even grass clippings. Peat moss is best worked lightly into the surface of the soil; otherwise, it is apt to form a crust.

"Rose plants are susceptible to black spot, mildew and the ravages of insects. It is advisable, therefore, to dust or spray rose plants at least once a week. Regular applications are necessary, covering both upper and under sides of the foliage. A well-nourished rose plant is more likely to resist disease than a weakened one. Any of the well-balanced commercially prepared rose food will stimulate growth and bloom. It should be applied around the base of the plants at intervals of about three weeks and watered in well. It is not advisable to fertilize rose plants after September first."

43. Watering of roses is the least important of the measures to be taken to insure good rose bloom.

44. Moisture should go down around the rose plant to a depth of about three inches.

45. Removing the nozzle from the hose and letting the water trickle into the soil is a method of getting water to the roots of the plants.

46. The roots of rose plants will be protected against heat, cold and draught by a four-inch layer of mulch on the surface of the soil.

47. Grass clippings are not suitable as a mulch for roses.

48. Peat moss not worked into the surface of the soil is apt to form a crust.

49. Rose plants are susceptible to black spot and mildew.

50. Rose plants should not be dusted or sprayed more than once a month.

51. It is necessary to apply a spray or dust on the under side of the foliage only.

52. A rose plant is more likely to resist disease if it is well nourished.

53. A well-balanced commercially prepared rose food will stimulate growth and bloom of the rose plant.

54. The rose food should be applied to the plant once during the growing season.

55. Rose plants should be fertilized up to November first.

Your answers to questions 56 to 62 must be based only on the information given in the following paragraph and not upon any other information you may have.

"In dry weather, after a few minutes of light sprinkling, the surface soil may become muddy and the inexperienced gardener is fooled into believing that enough water has been applied. Actually the water may not even reach the roots. The roots may be in an almost powdery dry earth below a thin layer of mud from which the water quickly evaporates. Deep roots thus get no benefit while shallow roots are attracted to the upper surface of the soil and are worse off than if no sprinkling had been done. Sprinkling should always be continued on any one spot until the soil has become drenched. The best time of the day to sprinkle is toward or during the evening because usually the air is cooler and evaporation losses will be reduced to a minimum."

56. A few minutes of light sprinkling in dry weather may make the surface of the soil become muddy.

57. After a few minutes of light sprinkling in dry weather the water may not even reach the roots.

58. Deep roots get no benefit from a light sprinkling.

59. Shallow roots are better off with a light sprinkling than with no sprinkling.

60. Sprinkling should not be continued on any one spot for so long that the soil becomes drenched.

61. The best time of day to sprinkle is toward or during evening.

62. The least amount of evaporation loss occurs during the evening because the air is usually cooler then.

63. "Some plants are grown for the decorative value of their leaves." In this sentence, the word 'decorative' means nearly the same as 'ornamental'.

64. "They made a circular flower garden." In this sentence, the word 'circular' means nearly the same as 'square'.

65. "The gardener was a conscientious worker." In this sentence, the word 'conscientious' means nearly the same as 'lazy.'

66. "A decaying branch is dangerous to the life of a tree." In this sentence the word 'decaying' means nearly the same as 'rotting.'

67. "Shearing helps keep the plants in the shape required." In this sentence the word 'shearing' means nearly the same as 'watering.'

68. "Some shrubs have vigorous growth and early flowering." In this sentence, the word 'vigorous' means nearly the same as 'weak.'

69. "The lawn retained its healthy green color." In this sentence, the word 'retained' means nearly the same as 'kept.'

70. "The soil is combined with an acid plant food." In this sentence, the word 'combined' means nearly the same as 'mixed.'

71. "Gardening can be tiring without the right tools." In this sentence, the word 'tiring' means nearly the same as 'amusing.'

72. "With the ground saturated the roots may die." In this sentence, the word 'saturated' means nearly the same as 'soaked.'

73. "Air can penetrate freely if holes are made in the soil." In this sentence, the word 'penetrate' means nearly the same as 'escape.'

74. "With some plants flowers precede the growth of leaves." In this sentence, the word 'precede' means nearly the same as 'follow.'

75. "The gardener anticipated frost." In this sentence, the word 'anticipated' means nearly the same as 'expected.'

76. "Tools are assembled when the job is finished." In this sentence, the word 'assembled' means nearly the same as 'cleaned.'

77. "Part of the area was set aside for a miniature rock garden." In this sentence, the word 'miniature' means nearly the same as 'beautiful.'

78. "Cheap tools are seldom durable." In this sentence, the word 'durable' means nearly the same as 'long lasting.'

79. "Concrete walks are maintained clean easily." In this sentence, the word 'maintained' means nearly the same as 'kept.'

80. "Each morning the gardener was punctual in reporting to work." In this sentence, the word 'punctual' means nearly the same as 'prompt.'

81. "The landscaping work was a prolonged task." In this sentence, the word 'prolonged' means nearly the same as 'difficult.'

82. "A transparent removable cover was placed over the flower bed." In this sentence, the word 'transparent' means nearly the same as 'wooden.'

83. The present New York City sales tax is 8¼ per cent.

84. The Comptroller of the City of New York is appointed by the Mayor.

85. The President of the City Council is elected by a majority vote of the members of the City Council.

86. A good part of the money needed to run the city government comes out of taxes on real estate.

87. The population of New York City is less than 6 million.

88. Dr. Jonas E. Salk developed the anti-polio vaccine.

89. The Police Commissioner of New York City is appointed by the Mayor for a five year period.

90. New York City is made up of six boroughs.

91. The fees for auto license registration are paid to the state.

92. City income taxes are collected by New York State.

93. A member of the local law-making body is known as an alderman.

94. If a group of assistant gardeners planted 1,278 plants in zone A, 1,262 plants in zone B, 1,020 plants in zone C and 793 plants in zone D, then the total number of plants planted by this group in these 4 zones was between 4,450 to 4,500.

95. If a gardener assigned to a job does 1/3 of the work on Monday, 1/3 of the work on Wednesday and the remainder on Friday, then the part of the work done by him on Friday is 1/3 of the whole job.

96. If a gardener can dig up 150 sq. yds. of lawn area every 3 hours, then in 5 hours he can dig up 350 sq. yds. of lawn area.

97. If a gardener rejects 12 spades out of a total shipment of 48, then the number of spades that he rejected is 25% of the total.

98. If 4 gardeners planted a total of 60 shrubs a day for a period of 22 days, then the total number of shrubs planted by these 4 was between 1,300 and 1,400.

99. If a park department spent $14.50 for rose bushes, $76.15 for lawn seed, $20.00 for lime and $36.80 for tulip bulbs, then the total amount of money spent by the department was $137.45.

100. If 165 plants are distributed equally among 15 parks, then each park will get 11 plants.

## Answer Key

| | | | | |
|---|---|---|---|---|
| 1. T | 21. T | 41. F | 61. T | 81. F |
| 2. T | 22. F | 42. T | 62. T | 82. F |
| 3. F | 23. F | 43. F | 63. T | 83. T |
| 4. F | 24. F | 44. F | 64. F | 84. F |
| 5. F | 25. T | 45. T | 65. F | 85. F |
| 6. T | 26. T | 46. T | 66. T | 86. T |
| 7. T | 27. T | 47. F | 67. F | 87. F |
| 8. F | 28. T | 48. T | 68. F | 88. T |
| 9. T | 29. F | 49. T | 69. T | 89. T |
| 10. F | 30. T | 50. F | 70. T | 90. F |
| 11. T | 31. T | 51. F | 71. F | 91. T |
| 12. T | 32. F | 52. T | 72. T | 92. T |
| 13. T | 33. T | 53. T | 73. F | 93. F |
| 14. F | 34. T | 54. F | 74. F | 94. F |
| 15. T | 35. F | 55. F | 75. T | 95. T |
| 16. F | 36. T | 56. T | 76. F | 96. F |
| 17. T | 37. F | 57. T | 77. F | 97. T |
| 18. T | 38. T | 58. T | 78. T | 98. T |
| 19. F | 39. T | 59. F | 79. T | 99. F |
| 20. T | 40. T | 60. F | 80. T | 100. T |

# SAMPLE PRACTICE EXAMINATION VI

DIRECTIONS FOR ANSWERING QUESTIONS

Answer all questions. Each question consists of a statement. You are to decide whether the statement is true or false. Mark the letter "T" if the statement is true or correct; mark the letter "F" if the statement is false or wrong.

The time allowed for the entire examination is 3 hours.

1. Fence posts sunk into the soil need no wood preservative below the soil line because the earth itself is a natural preservative.

2. A gardener who sees a man drop papers on a lawn should say nothing and pick the papers up himself in order to keep the goodwill of the public.

3. One reason for wrapping newly planted trees with burlap cloth when they are over 2 inches in diameter is to cut down on loss of water through the bark of the tree.

4. When a large branch is cut from a tree-like shrub, the cut should usually be left open to the healing powers of the air.

5. If you find that a lawn area your supervisor has sent you to mow has just been mowed by another gardener, you should say nothing and mow the lawn anyway.

6. A sandy soil usually holds water longer than a clay soil.

7. Pole pruners are used mainly for sawing down posts.

8. A fan-shaped bamboo rake is a good rake for gathering leaves on a lawn.

9. If your foreman asks you to help a gang of laborers who are digging a trench, you should refuse to do so because digging is not one of the duties of a gardener.

10. Before using a chisel that has "mushroomed" from constant use, a gardener should lay the chisel on a hard piece of steel and hammer the "mushroomed" edges until they disappear.

11. If you wish to dig up a plant in order to replant it, you should do this on a sunny day so that the roots receive sunlight they seldom get.

12. Lime is usually added to the soil to make the soil more acidic.

13. The leaf is usually the part of the plant that makes food for the plant.

14. Gasoline is one of the safest cleaning liquids to use for greasy and dirty metal equipment.

15. A gardener should work steadily but slowly so that there will be enough work to go around.

16. When a dump truck brings brush to a spot to be burned, the truck should usually dump the brush at a place some distance from the fire rather than right on the fire.

17. If the sod you are cutting for replanting seems to be infected with fungus, you should report this to your foreman as soon as possible.

18. The best trees for planting on streets are those with roots that can get into sewers for water.

19. To let sunlight get to the lower branches, a hedge should usually be trimmed so that it is wider at the top than at the bottom.

20. To help grass on a lawn become deeply rooted, it is better to soak the lawn with water when needed than to water it lightly every day.

21. If you overhear several teenagers plotting a gang fight in the park to which you are assigned, you should notify your supervisor so that she can take action.

22. Most northern grasses should be cut much shorter than usual in a summer drought because shorter grass leaves require less water.

23. You notice that a mechanic working in the park is doing his work in a way you consider inefficient. You, as the gardener, should report this mechanic for inefficiency.

24. A newly planted bed of lawn seed should be watered with a fine spray rather than a heavy spray to keep from washing the seed away.

25. A scythe is mainly used to trim hedges.

26. If you see a child annoying squirrels in the park, you should call a police officer to arrest the child.

27. A sickle is mainly used to cut tall grass and weeds.

Your answers to questions 28 to 36 must be based only on the information given in the following paragraph and not on any other information you may have.

"Plant reproduction is called propagation. Methods of propagation are divided into two classes, those methods which depend on seed and those depending on the use of buds. Buds are the small swellings on plant stems from which shoots, clusters of leaves, or flowers develop. Propagation by seed is called sexual, propagation by buds called asexual. Asexual propagation depends primarily upon the activity of the cambium. This is a layer of very thin tissue consisting entirely of young, easily broken cells filled with protoplasm, the basic stuff found in all living things. This cambium layer forms new plant tissues under the proper circumstances. It plays an important part in growth, in healing, and in asexual reproduction. When a bud is cut from a parent plant and inserted into water, sand, or other material suitable for starting growth, the cambium promotes root formation on the bud. When a branch is cut from one tree and grafted onto another of the same kind, the cambium from the branch unites with that of the tree and develops an additional protective covering. Propagation by asexual rather than sexual means is used because it is the most certain means of producing an offspring closely resembling the parent."

28. One example of propagation by sexual means is the growing of a plant from a bud.

29. Several forms of growth can develop from buds on a plant stem.

30. The cambium layer is made up of tough cells that help protect the tree.

31. A special quality of the cambium layer is that it will form new plant tissues under any circumstances.

32. Cambium activity is important in asexual reproduction.

33. All living animals have protoplasm in them.

34. Roots may start to grow from a bud cut from a parent plant only when the bud is placed in sand.

35. When a branch from one tree is grafted onto another tree of the same kind, the cambium of the first tree joins with that of the second.

36. The surest way of obtaining plants that look very much like the parent plant is to grow such plants from the seeds of the parent.

Your answers to questions 37 to 41 must be based only on the information given in the following paragraph and not on any other information you may have.

"The soil around young trees and shrubs is often cultivated the first two or three years in order to insure a good start. Cultivation helps to control and eliminate weeds but has no other value in stimulating plant growth. Deep cultivation is done in the spring. As the growing season progresses, cultivation should be gradually shallower. This method may result in the destruction of feeding roots formed the previous year in the same cultivated areas, but it does not disturb the carrier roots from which the feeding roots came. If the tree or shrub is not cultivated for a few years, however, these feeding roots grow into carrier roots with feeding roots growing mainly from their ends. When cultivation is resumed after such an interval, extra precaution must be taken not to prune the carrier roots too severely. Injurious results of severe root pruning may be partially offset by a correspondingly severe pruning of the top at the time of root pruning."

37. Cultivating the earth around young trees for the first two or three years helps plant growth by letting air get to the roots.

38. Even though the method of cultivating a young tree may be the right one, some feeding roots of the tree may be destroyed.

39. Cultivation of young trees at the beginning of the growing season should be more shallow than cultivation late in the growing season.

40. If several seasons of growth of a tree have gone by without cultivation, some feeding roots grow into carrier roots.

41. Cutting a lot from the top of a tree makes up partly for the bad effects of cutting a lot from the roots.

Your answers to questions 42 to 46 must be based only on the information given in the following paragraph and not upon any other information you may have.

"Low shrubs need no guys to maintain their position. But newly planted trees and tree-like shrubs, unless they are staked or guyed at once, may be pushed out of alignment by the wind or other forces. When pulled by a wire back to a vertical position, such trees continue to exert a force against the pull. In such cases not only will all the strain usually be put on one stake or guy wire but, most important, air pockets may form around the roots. To best maintain the stability of the tree, the tension on all stakes and guy wires should be approximately equal at the time of planting. Although the tension on individual wires will then vary with the conditions met later, the position of the tree is not likely to be affected."

42. To keep the wind from bending low shrubs, they should be staked or guyed right after planting.

43. If a tree pushed out of line is then pulled straight by one wire, the chances are that the tree will snap back out of line if the wire is cut.

44. The most important result of guying straight a tree that has been knocked out of line is that most of the strain is usually put on one guy wire.

45. Straightening out a tree after it has been pushed from its vertical position helps to remove air pockets around the roots.

46. If three guy wires are used to support a small tree after planting, the tension on one guy wire should be approximately one third of the total tension on all three guy wires.

Your answers to questions 47 to 50 must be based only on the information in the following paragraph and not upon any other information you may have.

"Sun often injures trees by burning their trunks and main branches. Especially susceptible to such injury are those trees growing in well-cultivated orchards. In the Northern Hemisphere such injury usually occurs on the south side although it often also occurs on the east side, less often on the west and never on the north side. The damage is sometimes confined to these exposed bark areas, but such limitation to exposed bark areas only is seldom found. When the tissues in the inner bark are destroyed, the downward flow of plant food is impeded and the roots to which these tissues lead are deprived of nourishment."

47. One method of protecting trees from sun injury is to cultivate well the orchard in which they grow.

48. In the United States, one side of the tree on which sun injury usually occurs is the north side.

49. Sun damage to trees is sometimes restricted to the outer bark of the tree.

50. Root nourishment depends on the downward flow of plant food in the inner bark.

Your answers to questions 51 to 53 must be based only on information given in the following paragraph and not upon any other information you may have.

"The belt should always be taut when clutch is fully engaged and at no other time. To check the belt for proper tension, first start the engine, and then bear down lightly on the handle of the mower in order to raise the mower wheels off the ground. While in this position, engage the clutch; then stop the engine by shorting the sparkplug with the stop switch, leaving the clutch engaged. If the belt is not taut, loosen the nut which holds the countershaft pedestal in order to make the countershaft pedestal movable. Then slide the countershaft pedestal to the back to tighten the belt. Sliding the countershaft pedestal forward loosens the belt."

51. The only time the belt should be tight is when the clutch is engaged completely.

52. When testing the belt for correct tension the clutch should be engaged after the mower wheels are raised off the ground.

53. To make the belt looser, tighten the nut holding the countershaft pedestal.

Your answers to questions 54 to 60 must be based only on information given in the following paragraph and not upon any other information you may have.

"The soil around actively growing delphiniums should receive a thorough soaking at least once a week. Delphiniums can be transplanted either in the autumn or in the spring. The fine and fibrous root system of these plants facilitates their removal. Since delphiniums are among the first herbaceous plants to start growth in the spring, autumn transplanting is recommended because the plants then undoubtedly suffer less shock. If the work is done with extreme care it is possible to move quite large plants when they are just coming into bloom. Large plants must be lifted with a generous quantity of earth in order that the root system remain intact. The use of a plastic spray will prevent wilting if applied before the plants are moved."

54. Delphiniums must be watered more than once a week.

55. Delphiniums are difficult to remove because of their thick, tough roots.

56. Delphiniums start growth earlier in the spring than many other herbaceous plants.

57. Delphiniums experience more shock from transplanting in the spring than in the fall.

58. To keep the root system together when large delphiniums are moved, a large amount of earth should be taken up with the roots.

59. One way of preventing a delphinium from wilting when moved is to apply a plastic spray to the plant beforehand.

60. Large delphinium plants are most easily moved at the time they are beginning to bloom.

61. "Formal shearing destroys the plant's individuality." In this sentence, the word 'formal' means nearly the same as 'irregular.'

62. "The entire tree is covered with a film that is flexible, colorless, and lasting." In this sentence, the word 'flexible' means nearly the same as 'tough.'

63. "All of the equipment is mobile." In this sentence, the word 'mobile' means nearly the same as the word 'movable.'

64. "Just enough asphalt adheres to make a mat." In this sentence, the word 'adheres' means nearly the same as the word 'sticks.'

65. "Efforts at proper maintenance were nullified by this act." In this sentence, the word 'nullified' means nearly the same as 'brought to nothing.'

66. Saying that a hose is "perforated" is another way of saying that a hose is "bent."

67. "Do not injure the foliage of a plant" means nearly the same as "do not injure the plant's roots."

68. "Pulverizing" soil is breaking it down into very small bits.

69. Humus is the part of the soil very often called clay in gardening practice.

70. "Aerating" a turf area is nearly the same as "sodding" the area.

71. "To mechanically agitate" means nearly the same as "to seed by mechanical power."

72. "To eliminate hand pumping" means nearly the same as "to do away with hand pumping."

73. "Discarding a ladder with a cracked rung" means nearly the same as "repairing a ladder with a cracked rung."

74. A "projecting" stub is usually a stub which sticks out.

75. A "nitrogen deficiency" in the soil is an oversupply of nitrogen in the soil.

76. Saying that a soil has a heavy "texture" is nearly the same as saying that the soil has a deep color.

77. A "neutral" soil is one in which no useful plants will grow.

78. A plant that is "dormant" is usually in an inactive period of growth.

79. Saying that sun is "detrimental" to ferns is nearly the same as saying that sun is harmful to ferns.

80. "Vendors are permitted only in certain park areas." In this sentence, the word 'vendors' means nearly the same as 'sellers.'

81. Residents of New York City pay a federal sales tax.

82. The largest zoo in New York City is located in Bronx Park.

83. The Police Commissioner of the City of New York is an elected official.

84. The Mayor of the City of New York is empowered to perform marriages.

85. The New York City governmental body that makes local laws for New York City is commonly known as the Legislature.

86. The administrators of most city agencies are appointed by the Mayor.

87. All parks in New York State located outside New York City are state parks.

88. The Department of Consumer Affairs issues all licenses in the City of New York.

89. All permanent New York City employees are required to join a retirement system.

90. The New York City Aquarium is located in Battery Park, Manhattan.

91. If 100 lbs. of a certain artificial fertilizer does a job equal to that done by 1 ton of a certain kind of manure, then 125 lbs. of this fertilizer should do the same job as 1½ tons of the manure.

92. If a gardener digs up an average of 73 sq. yds. of lawn area per hour, then the total area dug up in eight hours by this gardener should be 574 sq. yds.

93. From a total of 245 shrubs in a nursery, 56 shrubs are taken away the first day and 62 shrubs are brought into the nursery on the second day. The number of shrubs in the nursery at the beginning of the third day should be 251.

94. A gardener finished 1/3 of a job on the first day, 1/2 of the job on the second day, and the balance on the third day. The part of the job done by the assistant gardener on the third day was equal to the part done on the first day.

95. If there are 231 cubic inches in a gallon, then in 1/3 of a gallon there are 77 cubic inches.

96. If 12½% of a total force of 8,080 employees are laborers, then there are 1,010 laborers in this force.

97. If a bill for gardening materials lists $15.40 for rose bushes, $78.45 for lawn seed, $24.15 for fertilizer and $27.10 for bulbs and corms, then the total cost of these items is $145.10

98. A gardener must distribute a certain number of plants equally among a certain number of parks. To find the number of plants to give to each park, he should divide the number of parks by the number of plants.

99. A lawn 47 feet wide and 93 feet long has an area of 4,471 square feet.

100. If 14 out of a total of 114 shrubs are evergreens, then 14% of the total are evergreens.

## Answer Key

| | | | | |
|---|---|---|---|---|
| 1. F | 21. T | 41. T | 61. F | 81. F |
| 2. F | 22. F | 42. F | 62. F | 82. T |
| 3. T | 23. F | 43. T | 63. T | 83. T |
| 4. F | 24. T | 44. F | 64. T | 84. T |
| 5. F | 25. F | 45. F | 65. T | 85. F |
| 6. F | 26. F | 46. T | 66. F | 86. T |
| 7. F | 27. T | 47. F | 67. F | 87. F |
| 8. T | 28. F | 48. F | 68. T | 88. F |
| 9. F | 29. T | 49. T | 69. F | 89. T |
| 10. F | 30. F | 50. T | 70. F | 90. F |
| 11. F | 31. F | 51. T | 71. F | 91. F |
| 12. F | 32. T | 52. T | 72. T | 92. F |
| 13. T | 33. T | 53. F | 73. F | 93. T |
| 14. F | 34. F | 54. F | 74. T | 94. F |
| 15. F | 35. T | 55. F | 75. F | 95. T |
| 16. T | 36. F | 56. T | 76. F | 96. T |
| 17. T | 37. F | 57. T | 77. F | 97. T |
| 18. F | 38. T | 58. T | 78. T | 98. F |
| 19. F | 39. F | 59. T | 79. T | 99. F |
| 20. T | 40. T | 60. F | 80. T | 100. F |

# SAMPLE PRACTICE

# EXAMINATION VII

DIRECTIONS FOR ANSWERING QUESTIONS

Answer all questions. Each question consists of a statement. You are to decide whether the statement is true or false. Mark the letter "T" if the statement is true or correct; mark the letter "F" if the statement is false or wrong.

Time allowed for entire examination is 3 hours.

1. Weeds are usually undesirable in a lawn because they take away plant food from the good grasses.

2. When flowering shrubs are planted they should be crowded very close together so that weeds will not have room to grow.

3. It is usually good practice to spade the soil when wet because it is easier to work when it is in that condition.

4. The size of a hole in which a piece of nursery stock is to be planted should be determined by the time available to dig the hole rather than by the size of the plant and its roots.

5. Lawn clippings that are not too heavy may be left on a lawn after the lawn is mowed.

6. Chemical fertilizers in powdered form should be applied to a lawn on a windy day so that the wind will blow them into the ground.

7. To prevent rust, it is usually good practice to put a coat of oil on garden tools when they are stored away for the winter.

8. When she transplants a plant from one place in the garden to another, the gardener should be careful to avoid injury to the roots.

9. Freshly planted nursery stock is often pruned by cutting off part of the branches. The main purpose of this pruning is usually to keep the plant from growing further.

10. Chemical sprays are often used to kill insect enemies of plants.

11. The purpose of adding chemical fertilizers to the soil is usually to provide additional plant food.

12. A gardener who does not know all the latest developments in gardening will not be able to do his work properly.

13. It is good practice to keep the cutting edge of a garden tool slightly dull in order to prevent injury to the user of the tool.

14. A gardener who is given a job she does not know how to do should ask for further instructions.

15. A shrub planted by a gardener fails to grow. This proves that the shrub was not planted correctly.

16. Some garden insects are beneficial to plant life and should not be killed.

17. Plants must have light in order to grow properly.

18. If a gardener accidentally sticks the point of a sharp tool into the bark of a tree, the tree will die within a few years.

19. During a long dry spell it is advisable to water carefully recently planted nursery stock.

20. An important reason why a gardener should know the proper use of each garden tool is that if he uses a tool improperly he may spoil it.

21. A gardener should carry out her superior's orders only if she knows that the orders are correct according to the best gardening practice.

22. Whenever he suffers a slight cut or scratch while at work, a gardener should immediately go to the nearest doctor to be treated.

23. A gardener who always finds a lot of rubbish in the park area to which she is assigned should issue a warning to every person who uses the area.

24. If a passerby asks a gardener who is at work in a park for directions on how to get to another part of the park, the gardener should refer him to the

nearest policeman so that his work will not be interrupted.

25. A gardener should never help a fellow employee with her work unless he has received permission in writing from the supervisor.

26. A gardener is assigned a job by her supervisor and told that it must be finished by a certain time. If, after working on the job for a while, the gardener is sure that she will not be able to finish on time she should immediately let her supervisor know.

27. You have an unwrapped shrub with bare roots that you are ready to plant when you receive a call to go to another part of the park. Before you leave, it would be advisable for you to temporarily cover the roots of the plant with soil so as to prevent them from drying out.

28. After plants are established and growing they require no further attention.

Your answers to questions 29 to 33 must be based only on the information given in the following paragraph and not upon any other information you may have.

"To insure thick growth from the ground up, hedges should be cut back to a few inches from the ground when planted. The properly shaped hedge is narrower at the top than at the bottom, and the top should be rounded rather than flat. The sloping sides admit much light to the lower branches. A somewhat narrow and rounded top also sheds snow instead of accumulating a heavy load and sometimes bending or breaking it."

29. Hedges should be cut down to a few inches from the ground after they have grown dense at the bottom.

30. Trimming of hedges should be done in such a way as to give them a rounded top.

31. A hedge shaped wider at the top than at the bottom will admit much light to the bottom branches.

32. Snow will tend to accumulate and stay on a hedge with a wide, flat top.

33. A hedge can sometimes be broken by the weight of the snow accumulated on top of it.

Your answers to questions 34 to 43 must be based only on the information given in the following paragraph and not upon any other information you may have.

"Arsenate of lead, the best known and most widely used stomach poison, comes in two forms, basic and acid. The basic form is less likely to burn tender growth but stays in suspension poorly and kills insects more slowly. Most commercial preparations are the acid form usually sold as a powder, sometimes as a paste. For general spraying use the powder at the rate of 3 lbs. to 100 gallons of water; or in small quantitites, use one heaping tablespoon to one gallon of water. If the paste form is available, use twice the amount recommended."

34. There is an acid form and a basic form of arsenate of lead.

35. No stomach poison is better known than arsenate of lead.

36. No other stomach poison is used as much as arsenate of lead.

37. The basic form of arsenate of lead kills insects more quickly than the acid form.

38. There are many forms of arsenate of lead.

39. The basic form of arsenate of lead is more likely to burn plants than the acid form.

40. The acid form of arsenate of lead is usually sold as a paste.

41. Commercially prepared arsenate of lead is usually of the acid form.

42. The paste of the acid form of arsenate of lead, when used for general spraying, should be mixed at the rate of 3 lbs. to 100 gallons of water.

43. The powder of the acid form of arsenate of lead, when used for general spraying, should be used at the rate of one heaping teaspoon to a gallon of water.

Your answers to questions 44 to 53 must be based only on the information given in the following paragraph and not upon any other information you may have.

"A commercial fertilizer may be a single substance such as nitrate of soda, or it may be a combination of such materials that contains a definite ratio of the three main plant-food elements, nitrogen, phosphorus and potassium. Such a mixture is said to be complete. If the proportions of the three elements are such as to meet the full needs of a certain plant, the fertilizer is said to be balanced as well as complete. As the plant food compounds in commercial fertilizers are in highly soluble form they should not be applied too heavily nor allowed to come in contact with plant parts. Small frequent applications are safest and least wasteful as they give less chance for the soluble salts to be dissolved and leached out of the soil before the plant roots can get them. It is usually advisable to water the soil after adding commercial fertilizer, both to put the fertilizer in solution so that the plants can take it up and to prevent the fertilizer from absorbing the moisture in the soil."

44. All commercial fertilizers consist of a combination of the three main plant food elements.

45. Nitrate of soda is available as a commercial fertilizer.

46. The three main plant food elements are nitrate of soda, nitrogen, and phosphorus.

47. A complete fertilizer contains nitrogen, potassium and phosphorus.

48. Any fertilizer which contains nitrogen, potassium and phosphorus is said to be balanced.

49. The plant food elements in commercial fertilizers are very soluble.

50. A commercial fertilizer should be mixed right in among the roots of a plant so that it becomes available quickly.

51. Commercial fertilizers should be applied to the soil in large amounts.

52. Commercial fertilizer must be in solution before it can be taken up by plants.

53. If the soil is not watered when commercial fertilizer is applied, the fertilizer may absorb moisture already in the soil.

Your answers to questions 54 to 68 must be based only on the information given in the following paragraph and not upon any other information you may have.

"Bent grass is the common name for Agrostis, a large class of mostly low growing and spreading grasses including some valuable, high class lawn grasses as well as the important pasture grass, redtop. Bent grasses are annual or perennial, have somewhat rough, flat or slightly rolled leaves and bear loose panicles of small reddish flowers. While some of the forms are grown from seed, those used for fine lawns and golf courses are of the creeping type and are increasingly being grown from stolons, which are simply the chopped-up stems. Bent grasses will do well in sun or partial shade, but are not in any sense a shady-spot variety. The soil should be well supplied with thoroughly rotted manure and receive a good application of a balanced complete fertilizer before planting time. In sowing, use about one pound of seed to 250 square feet; if stolons are used, broadcast them at the rate of 25 square feet of stolons to 200 square feet of area. They must then be covered lightly with soil, rotted and watered."

54. Agrostis is the common name for bent grass.

55. Redtop is a pasture grass.

56. Agrostis is a variety of redtop.

57. Most bent grasses are low growing.

58. Not all bent grasses are perennial.

59. All bent grasses are annual.

60. Bent grasses bear flowers.

61. Creeping bent grasses are used on golf courses.

62. All bent grass lawns are grown from seed.

63. A stolon is a chopped-up bent grass seed.

64. Bent grasses are good for planting in heavily shaded areas.

65. Before bent grass is planted, rotted manure and a balanced complete fertilizer should be added to the soil.

66. Bent grass may be sown at the rate of 1/2 pound of seed to 125 square feet.

67. When bent grass is planted by means of stolons, 25 pounds of stolons should be broadcast to 200 square feet of area.

68. After being broadcast, stolons should be covered with at least three inches of soil.

69. "The instructions received were contradictory." In this sentence, the word 'contradictory' means nearly the same as 'alike.'

70. "His application for the job was rejected." In this sentence, the word 'rejected' means nearly the same as 'accepted.'

71. "This plant reaches maturity quickly." In this sentence, the word 'maturity' means nearly the same as 'full development.'

72. "The garden was provided with a system of underground irrigation." In this sentence, the word 'irrigation' means nearly the same as 'watering.'

73. "In some plants, the flowers often appear before the foliage." In this sentence, the word 'foliage' refers to the leaves of the plant.

74. "The new horticultural society was organized through the merger of two previous groups." In this sentence, the word 'merger' means nearly the same as 'breakup.'

75. "The stem of the plant measured three inches in diameter." In this sentence, the word 'diameter' means nearly the same as 'height.'

76. "For proper growth the plant needs plenty of water, supplemented with liquid manure." In this sentence, the word 'supplemented' means nearly the same as 'replaced.'

77. "One reason why aphids are undesirable is that they transmit plant diseases." In this sentence, the word 'transmit' means nearly the same as 'pass on.'

78. "When the trees are young, the spaces between them may be utilized for other plantings." In this sentence, the word 'utilized' means nearly the same as 'used.'

79. "The cuttings will take root readily." In this sentence, the word 'readily' means nearly the same as 'quickly.'

80. "The seedlings should be transplanted at least once to stimulate growth." In this sentence, the word 'stimulate' means nearly the same as 'encourage.'

81. If you see a new employee doing a job the wrong way you should show him the right way.

82. If your supervisor gives you an assignment which you do not like you should ask her to assign another employee to this work.

83. If your supervisor gives you instructions for a job which you do not understand, you should do the job the best you can and not take up his time by asking him to explain the instructions.

84. A new employee can sometimes learn how to do a job just by watching an experienced employee do the job.

85. If you cannot get along with a fellow employee the proper thing for you to do is to ask your supervisor to transfer this employee to another assignment.

86. Even though a gardener has had gardening experience before coming to the city, a short period of training in city methods and procedures would probably be helpful.

87. If you know in advance that you will not be able to come to work on a certain day you should telephone your supervisor at about 11 o'clock on the morning of that day.

88. At the end of the working day only those tools that are not going to be used the next day should be put back in their regular storage place.

89. If some work that you did is criticized by your supervisor because of mistakes you made, you should try to avoid these mistakes the next time you do such work.

90. Your supervisor instructs you to do a job in a certain way but you believe that there is a better way to do this job. You should disregard the supervisor's instructions and do the job in your own way.

91. If you are assigned to a job by your supervisor and given a time to complete it and you find you will be unable to, you should say nothing to your supervisor but you should ask a gardener working nearby to help you.

Your answers to questions 92 to 100 must be based solely on the information contained in the following quotation and not upon any other information you may have.

"Before laying sod prepare the soil as in making a lawn: rake it smooth and leave it, when loose and uncompacted, just about as high as the desired finished level. Lay the sods carefully, first along the margin of the area, then side by side toward the center. Fit the edges close together, adding or removing a little soil beneath as may be necessary to produce a level surface. When an area a few sods wide is laid, pound it down hard, using a heavy flat wooden block on a handle or the back of a spade. A plank should be laid to walk on while doing this so as to avoid making footprints in the new turf. Do not attempt to roll the sod but pound it well, especially where the edges join. Then soak it thoroughly."

92. After a piece of sod has been laid it should be stamped down with the feet or with a heavy flat wooden block on a handle.

93. To allow for expansion as a result of pounding, a very small space should be left between individual pieces of sod when they are laid.

94. An area on which sod is to be laid should be prepared in the same way as an area which is to be seeded for a lawn.

95. Rolling the sod after laying, especially where the edges join, is desirable.

96. The level of an area that has been prepared for the laying of sod should be about the same as the final level that is desired after the sod has been laid.

97. A spade is sometimes used in one of the operations connected with the laying of sod.

98. If when a piece of sod is laid down it is lower than the piece next to it, some additional soil should be put under it to bring it to the necessary level.

99. After the sod has been laid and pounded down, it is desirable to give it a good watering.

100. In laying sod over a prepared area, the best procedure to follow is to start in the center of the area and work outwards, laying the sods side by side.

## Answer Key

| | | | | |
|---|---|---|---|---|
| 1. T | 21. F | 41. T | 61. T | 81. T |
| 2. F | 22. F | 42. F | 62. F | 82. F |
| 3. F | 23. F | 43. F | 63. F | 83. F |
| 4. F | 24. F | 44. F | 64. F | 84. T |
| 5. T | 25. F | 45. T | 65. T | 85. F |
| 6. F | 26. T | 46. F | 66. T | 86. T |
| 7. T | 27. T | 47. T | 67. F | 87. F |
| 8. T | 28. F | 48. F | 68. F | 88. F |
| 9. F | 29. F | 49. T | 69. F | 89. T |
| 10. T | 30. T | 50. F | 70. F | 90. F |
| 11. T | 31. F | 51. F | 71. T | 91. F |
| 12. F | 32. T | 52. T | 72. T | 92. F |
| 13. F | 33. T | 53. T | 73. T | 93. F |
| 14. T | 34. T | 54. F | 74. F | 94. T |
| 15. F | 35. T | 55. T | 75. F | 95. F |
| 16. T | 36. T | 56. F | 76. F | 96. T |
| 17. T | 37. F | 57. T | 77. T | 97. T |
| 18. F | 38. F | 58. T | 78. T | 98. T |
| 19. T | 39. F | 59. F | 79. T | 99. T |
| 20. T | 40. F | 60. T | 80. T | 100. F |

# SAMPLE PRACTICE EXAMINATION VIII

DIRECTIONS FOR ANSWERING QUESTIONS

Answer all questions. Each question consists of a statement. You are to decide whether the statement is true or false. Mark the letter "T" if the statement is true or correct; mark the letter "F" if the statement is false or wrong.

Time allowed for the entire examination is 3 hours.

1. The poplar tree has a tendency to damage water mains.

2. The black locust tree is not likely to be affected if planted in a factory district often full of smoke fumes.

3. The roots of a silver maple tree tend to break into water mains.

4. A sugar maple tree is most likely to grow well in city streets.

5. Lime-sulfur is often successfully used as a winter spray.

6. Leaf-eating insects are likely to be controlled by using a spray of arsenate of lead.

7. The most successful way of treating a black locust tree that has been attacked by the locust borer is by spraying it with arsenate of lead.

8. Aphids, which are leaf sucking insects, can be eliminated by using a spray with Black Leaf 40.

9. Arsenate of lead is not used for sucking insects because it damages the leaves.

10. Scale insects require stronger poison than other insects.

11. The poplar tree loses its leaves late in the fall.

12. Contact poisons are harmless to leaf-eating insects.

13. The silver maple often grows where more beautiful trees do not.

14. A heavy spray of water is likely to wash the seeds away from a newly planted bed.

15. An application of aluminum sulfate is most efficient in reducing the acidity of soil.

16. A dibble is an uprooted sod.

17. The standard steel rake is adapted to all raking duties.

18. The hoe is specially adapted to open furrows.

19. Ordinarily an emery or a carborundum wheel is used to develop a new edge on garden tools.

20. A saw with teeth on both edges is most satisfactory for pruning in close quarters.

21. The term "fertilizer" is synonymous with plant food.

22. Lime has no direct plant food value.

23. Manure is one of the three principal plant food elements.

24. Plants need phosphorus to ripen the seed.

25. Hardwood ashes are good sources of potash.

26. Humus improves the soil texture by making it friable.

27. Barnyard manure is very desirable in preparing lawns.

28. Kentucky bluegrass is standard for a neutral loam in a sunny location.

29. Redtop is sometimes referred to as a nursery grass.

30. Bent grasses prefer an acid soil.

31. The fescues prefer moist soils.

32. A stolon is a sod of bent grass.

33. A small quantity of white clover in a grass mixture helps keep weeds out.

34. Early fall is a particularly good time to seed lawns.

35. Late spring is a particularly good time to feed lawns.

36. Sodium chloride kills ground ivy without causing lasting injury to grass.

37. Snowmold is a type of winter grass.

38. Lead arsenate is used to grub-proof new lawns.

39. The plant disease known as die-back refers to the rotting at the base of seedlings.

40. Mosaic is a plant disease typified by mottling or uneven color.

41. In the control of plant disease, the expression "eradication" means the disinfecting of seeds or plants before planting.

42. Aphids destroy plant life by chewing.

43. Plants propagated by cuttings are apt to revert to a previous type.

44. Dahlias may be propagated by layering.

45. Sprinkling new transplants is never advisable.

46. Plants with tap roots transplant with difficulty.

47. Shrubs are usually transplanted while dormant.

48. A compost of oak leaves tends to be alkaline.

49. The aspidistra, as a house plant, requires good soil and sunlight.

50. A coldframe becomes a hot bed when artificially heated.

Each of the items numbered 51 to 55 in Column I is a plant condition which is generally treated by one of the insecticides or fungicides listed in Column II. For each item in Column I, mark the insecticide in Column II used to treat the specific plant condition.

| Column I | Column II |
|---|---|
| 51. crown rot | (A) arsenate of lead in mixture |
| 52. mildew | (B) naphthalene flakes |
| 53. green aphids | (C) bordeaux mixture |
| 54. elm leaf beetle | (D) nicotine sulphate |
| 55. gladiolus thrips | |

The following list of standard shrubs may be divided into two groups: (A) summer or autumn flowering shrubs, the flower buds being formed on new wood the same year they blossom; and (B) spring and early summer flowering shrubs, the buds on which were formed the year before.

56. althea
57. lycium
58. azalea
59. rhododendron
60. spiraea bumalda
61. rose-acacia
62. deutzia
63. weigela
64. forsythia
65. hydrangea paniculata

The following list of perennials may be divided into two groups: (A) those most suitable for edging borders or in rock gardens, and (B) those most suitable for use as climbers. For each of the questions 66 to 75, mark the letter A if it is an edging or rock garden plant, and the letter B if it is a climbing plant.

66. sweet alyssum
67. ampelopsis
68. bignonia
69. primrose
70. heuchera
71. common hop
72. myosotis
73. wisteria
74. candytuft
75. clematis

The following list of annuals includes a number of climbing plants, as well as a number of low-growing plants. For each of the questions 76 to 81 mark (T) if it is a climbing annual, and (F) if it is not.

76. moonflower
77. african daisy
78. baby's breath
79. tom thumb nasturtium
80. pansy
81. sweet pea

The following list of plants may be divided into two groups: (A) those which require acid soil conditions for best growth, and (B) those which require alkaline soil conditions. For each of the Questions 82 to 87 inclusive, mark (A) if the plant requires acid soil, and (B) if it requires alkaline soil.

82. lady-slipper
83. clover
84. chrysanthemum
85. iris

86. phlox
87. mountain laurel

The following list of insects may be divided into two groups: (A) those which are harmful to plant life, and (B) those which are beneficial to plant life. For each of the Questions 88 to 92 inclusive, mark (A) if the insect is harmful to plant life, and (B) if it is beneficial to plant life.

88. dragon fly
89. flea beetle
90. ladybug beetle
91. mealy bug
92. praying mantis

Each of the items numbered 93 to 100 in Column I is a plant generally propagated by one of the methods listed in Column II. For each item in Column I, mark the letter in front of the method of propagation most appropriate for the plant

| Column I | Column II |
|---|---|
| 93. tulip | (A) bulb |
| 94. dahlia | (B) corm |
| 95. quackgrass | (C) tuber |
| 96. crocus | (D) rhizome |
| 97. jerusalem artichoke | |
| 98. gladiolus | |
| 99. hyacinth | |
| 100. solomon's seal | |

## Answer Key

| | | | | |
|---|---|---|---|---|
| 1. T | 21. F | 41. F | 61. B | 81. T |
| 2. T | 22. T | 42. F | 62. B | 82. A |
| 3. F | 23. F | 43. F | 63. B | 83. B |
| 4. F | 24. T | 44. F | 64. B | 84. A |
| 5. T | 25. T | 45. T | 65. A | 85. B |
| 6. T | 26. T | 46. T | 66. A | 86. B |
| 7. F | 27. F | 47. T | 67. B | 87. A |
| 8. T | 28. T | 48. F | 68. B | 88. B |
| 9. F | 29. T | 49. F | 69. A | 89. A |
| 10. T | 30. T | 50. T | 70. A | 90. B |
| 11. F | 31. F | 51. B | 71. B | 91. A |
| 12. F | 32. F | 52. C | 72. A | 92. B |
| 13. T | 33. T | 53. D | 73. B | 93. A |
| 14. T | 34. T | 54. A | 74. A | 94. C |
| 15. F | 35. F | 55. B | 75. B | 95. D |
| 16. F | 36. F | 56. A | 76. T | 96. B |
| 17. F | 37. F | 57. B | 77. F | 97. C |
| 18. T | 38. T | 58. B | 78. F | 98. B |
| 19. F | 39. F | 59. B | 79. F | 99. A |
| 20. F | 40. T | 60. A | 80. F | 100. D |

# Part Three

# *Job Related Study Material*

# SAFETY AT WORK

Accidents which occur at work are costly in many ways. They cause economic hardship to the injured workers in the form of time lost from work, medical expenses, and human suffering. They may deprive a family of its breadwinner. They are costly to the employer who has to replace a well-trained worker during the time the injured party is away from work. Accidents also raise the insurance rates of an organization. A smooth-running operation is likely to be upset. Therefore it is wise for an organization to devote sufficient time and effort to the prevention of accidents; it is effort well spent.

The majority of accidents can be avoided. They usually fall into one of two categories: those which may be attributed to carelessness either on the part of the injured or some other worker, or those caused by unsafe working conditions. A desk drawer or file drawer which is left open for another worker to trip over would be an example of the first type. An unsafe working condition may or may not be recognized by the employer, but even if it is safety precautions are often not taken either because of the expense involved or because speed of performance may have to be sacrificed for safety. Some employers hope that the expense of installing a safety device or control can be avoided. However, once an accident has occurred the employer soon realizes that he has acted foolishly because the cost of one accident is usually much greater than many safety devices which could have been installed to protect many workers.

Besides being expensive, accidents have an adverse effect on employee morale. Since employee morale, organizational efficiency, and production are directly related, one can readily see why progressive organizations, small and large alike, have seen fit to safeguard their workers while they are performing their duties.

When a worker sees accidents occurring around him he is likely to grow apprehensive. He will worry that he may fall victim to the next one. In an effort at self-protection he may slow down his working pace. Sad to say, however, overly cautious workers who perform their duties under unsafe conditions are not immune to accidents.

Modern personnel administration today recognizes that workers must perform their functions in an atmosphere permeated with safety precautions and that it is the responsibility of every employer to see that they do. Every organization should have a safety program to insure that accidents occurring on its premises will be kept to a minimum. The size of the program would depend upon the type of work being performed and the size of the organization. But even in the smallest organizations one man should be given the responsibility for looking after the safety of the workers. It would be his function to see to it that the safety aspects of all of the jobs are looked into and that sufficient safety guards are installed wherever a hazardous condition exists. The safety program should not be limited to locations where physical work is performed because a large number of accidents occur in offices, where one might think them highly unlikely.

It is believed by most experts in the field that there is a definite relationship between a worker's mental alertness and physical well-being and his involvement in accidents. A worker who permits his mind to wander to matters other than the work he is performing is more likely to become involved in an accident than a worker who gives his work his full concentration. A worker who is bothered by a physical ailment or who is not feeling up to par while performing his duties is also prone to accident involvement. Mentally alert workers seldom fall victim to industrial accidents. Their minds are fully occupied by the work they are doing. They are naturally careful and attentive to their surroundings.

It is impossible to implement a successful safety program without the cooperation and understanding of the workers. Signs can be posted throughout the plant attesting to the importance of the program, but if the workers are not convinced it is to their benefit to be alert and careful, they will not comply. Therefore it is imperative that every safety program, before it is implemented, have as one of its initial steps the indoctrination of the workers with the knowledge that work performance in a safe atmosphere will benefit them.

They must be shown how an accident is likely to cause them grief, economic hardship and may even interfere with their career. It is important that they understand the safety program is intended to protect their interests as well as those of the organization. A good method of getting them to accept a safety program is to permit a representative group of workers to have a say in its formation.

The responsibility for the formation of a safety program in an organization is one task that may be successfully delegated to a subordinate by the head of the agency. The individual who is chosen to conduct the safety program should be familiar with the intricacies of the various working units and should be allotted sufficient time and help to carry out a carefully planned program. Funds should be provided for the purchase of safety devices wherever necessary, and maintenance help should be provided to eliminate dangerous situations. Loose desk lamp wires, faulty file drawers, and overloaded top drawers of standing files are examples of dangerous situations which can be easily and quickly corrected.

The actual safety program should begin with a collection of all available data concerning accidents that have occurred in the past. This data should be carefully categorized and then analyzed. Much can be learned from this information which will aid in the prevention of similar accidents in the future. Enough time should be taken for this study so that definite conclusions may be reached as to the causes of the previous accidents. The safety officer must have some "meat" with which to begin his own program. The next step should be a concentrated effort to gain the cooperation and support of all of the workers in the program. The safety officer should also consult with the various supervisors and workers throughout the organization because much can be learned from those closest to the actual work.

One of the most important aspects of a safety program is its reporting system. A report must be filled out whenever an accident occurs no matter how insignificant it may be. These reports will provide the basis for the elimination of hazardous conditions. One individual in each unit should be held responsible for completion of such reports, and he should be adequately trained to do so properly. The workers must be convinced that the sole purpose of accident reports is to bring to light hazardous conditions which may be eliminated; otherwise they may attempt to cover up small accidents which then may lead to bigger ones at some later date. The report form should be designed with simplicity in mind, but it should call for enough information so that when completed, it will reflect the cause of the accident. The safety officer may find it necessary to conduct an investigation on his own in some instances, but most accident reports, if properly filled out, will form the basis for pinpointing the cause of an accident.

A safety program should be designed to bring to light hazardous conditions preferably before accidents occur, but in the event an accident does occur the program should move swiftly to eliminate the cause of the accident so that it does not happen once more.

Attractive posters designed to alert workers to avoid dangerous situations are an integral part of a safety program. They should be placed in work locations, locker rooms and areas where workers spend their breaks and eat their meals. The workers must constantly be reminded of the importance of safety. For example, posters depicting the proper way to lift heavy objects should be placed in strategic areas because the use of incorrect methods of lifting is the cause of many industrial accidents.

The final part of a safety program is the followup. It is the safety officer's job to see that his recommendations are implemented. This can prove to be quite a task. Supervisors have the job of producing maximum return from the labor and material afforded them. They may be reluctant to sacrifice speed for safety. Some supervisors may feel that "it can't happen here." The safety officer must therefore be extended sufficient authority to put his recommendations into effect. He should not resort to force, however, until absolutely necessary. The safety program will be much more beneficial if the supervisors and workers alike are convinced of its value and are willing to cooperate with the safety officer in putting his findings to work. Therefore the safety officer's job may involve some selling, too. A safety program is bound to be successful if the supervisors, workers, and safety officer all pull in the same direction.

## THE ACCIDENT-PRONE WORKER

Are individuals actually accident-prone? Are certain people more liable to involvement in accidents than others? Authorities are divided on the question. However, it is certain that some people become involved in a continuous stream of accidents while others avoid them almost entirely during their life span. Surely there are other factors besides lack of attentiveness and mental alertness while performing work that contribute to one's becoming involved in accidents. Some people avoid accidents by simply avoiding hazardous work situations. However, if a worker has a knack for becoming involved in accidents, how should he be treated? Should he be excused from work situations which involve any danger or should he be treated as all of the other workers are? The latest thinking on this subject places special emphasis on instructing workers who have multiple accident records. They should be taught how to work safely and to be safety conscious. An organization could not function properly if assignment of personnel were determined solely by the individual's accident record. A worker must perform at the job that will best suit the organization.

If a worker continues to become involved in accidents after he has been sufficiently trained and indoctrinated in safe work procedures, consideration should be given to discharging him. Most workers can avoid accidents if they put their minds to it. Special assignments for workers should only be made at the convenience of the organization.

## SAFETY AWARDS

Although abstinence from accidents is reward in itself for a working unit, most safety programs will also issue formal awards to accident-free groups in an organization. These awards are usually made in certificate form so that they can be displayed within the working area of a unit.

These awards are more accurately certificates of recognition. They serve to indicate that a working unit has recognized the value of safe working procedures to themselves and the organization alike. These units have seen fit to comply with the rules of safety in order to promote organizational efficiency and to rid the workers of an evil to which they do not have to fall victim.

These certificates of recognition tend to take on added importance in time. For a working unit not to possess a safety certificate may symbolize more than a poor safety record. It will indicate a lack of desire on the unit's part to do what has been deemed best for both themselves and the organization. The certificates will then become something that every unit will strive to attain to show that they want to "join the team." The competition for acquisition of safety certificates will indirectly achieve the result that the entire safety program was intended for: an accident-free organization with increased efficiency.

# PRACTICE QUESTIONS

| | | | |
|---|---|---|---|
| 1 Ⓐ Ⓑ Ⓒ Ⓓ | 6 Ⓐ Ⓑ Ⓒ Ⓓ | 11 Ⓐ Ⓑ Ⓒ Ⓓ | 16 Ⓐ Ⓑ Ⓒ Ⓓ |
| 2 Ⓐ Ⓑ Ⓒ Ⓓ | 7 Ⓐ Ⓑ Ⓒ Ⓓ | 12 Ⓐ Ⓑ Ⓒ Ⓓ | 17 Ⓐ Ⓑ Ⓒ Ⓓ |
| 3 Ⓐ Ⓑ Ⓒ Ⓓ | 8 Ⓐ Ⓑ Ⓒ Ⓓ | 13 Ⓐ Ⓑ Ⓒ Ⓓ | 18 Ⓐ Ⓑ Ⓒ Ⓓ |
| 4 Ⓐ Ⓑ Ⓒ Ⓓ | 9 Ⓐ Ⓑ Ⓒ Ⓓ | 14 Ⓐ Ⓑ Ⓒ Ⓓ | 19 Ⓐ Ⓑ Ⓒ Ⓓ |
| 5 Ⓐ Ⓑ Ⓒ Ⓓ | 10 Ⓐ Ⓑ Ⓒ Ⓓ | 15 Ⓐ Ⓑ Ⓒ Ⓓ | 20 Ⓐ Ⓑ Ⓒ Ⓓ |

1. If a new employee becomes involved in an accident he should be

   (A) given additional training in safe working methods
   (B) discharged immediately
   (C) held strictly responsible for the accident
   (D) no longer assigned to tasks where there is any danger involved

2. One of the workers under your supervision asks to be excused from performing a task on a particular day because it involves the use of a 12-foot ladder. He has performed this job before on numerous occasions, but he says he is not feeling just right today. You should

   (A) insist that he perform the function
   (B) tell him to find another worker who is willing to change places with him
   (C) assign the task to another employee this time
   (D) report him to your superior

3. If a worker continues to perform a job in an unsafe manner after he has been trained by his supervisor to perform it in the proper manner, he should be

   (A) permitted to perform the job in his own way because it is easier for him to do so
   (B) disciplined
   (C) praised because he has not yet become involved in an accident
   (D) once again retrained by his supervisor

4. In an accident report the <u>least</u> useful of the following information would be the

   (A) name of the injured worker
   (B) time and date accident occurred
   (C) length of time injured worker has been employed by the agency
   (D) extent of the injury

5. A supervisor who observes one of his subordinates performing his duties in an unsafe manner should

   (A) wait until the next staff meeting to correct him so that the whole staff will benefit
   (B) say nothing at the time, but wait until he observes him doing something else wrong to bring it up
   (C) have another subordinate correct him at the first opportunity
   (D) correct him at once

6. A report of an accident should be made as soon after the occurrence as practical chiefly because

   (A) the witnesses may change their stories before the report is written
   (B) the reporter should strive to rid himself of the chore so he can devote himself to more important work
   (C) the details of the accident will still be fresh in the reporter's mind
   (D) reports should be submitted promptly even if they do not contain all of the facts

7. If most accidents in a unit whose workers are performing routine work of a somewhat hazardous nature occur in the last hour of the workday, they are most likely due to

   (A) carelessness on the part of the workers
   (B) improper training of the workers
   (C) lack of interest in safety on the part of the workers
   (D) mental and physical fatigue on the part of the workers

8. If one of your subordinates approaches you, a supervisor, with the information that one of the functions he is performing may cause an accident, you should tell him

   (A) you are the supervisor and it is your function to determine work procedures
   (B) to put his information in writing
   (C) to refer the information to the safety officer
   (D) that you will investigate the matter at once

9. If, after completing a training course in safe work procedures, the trainees still continue to use the same procedures they used before attending the course

the most probable reason is that

(A) they were not convinced of the value of the procedures taught to them in the course
(B) they have not absorbed the training material
(C) the training material was not pertinent
(D) they are willing to engage in dangerous practices in order to get the work done quickly

10. If you, as a supervisor, observe a worker not under your jurisdiction performing his duties in an unsafe manner you should

(A) immediately instruct him in the proper method of work performance
(B) ignore him because the worker is not under your jurisdiction
(C) seek out his supervisor and inform him of his subordinate's action
(D) report the worker to the safety officer

11. If you observe what seems to be a serious accident to a worker in your unit, your first course of action should be to

(A) seek out the supervisor
(B) fill out an accident report
(C) notify the injured worker's family
(D) render any possible first aid to the victim

12. It is a poor practice to fill the top drawer of a file cabinet entirely before using the drawers beneath it chiefly because

(A) some file clerks may be shorter than others
(B) the cabinet will topple forward when the top drawer is opened entirely
(C) the file is not being used to its utmost capacity
(D) material should be distributed equally throughout the file

13. In order to avoid injuries it is proper to lift heavy objects

(A) with the knees bent and the back held stiff
(B) with both the knees and the back held stiff
(C) using the arms only
(D) in the manner best suited to the individual doing the lifting

14. The <u>least</u> likely reason for including a safety program in an organizational setup is

    (A) the type of work being performed
    (B) the number of workers employed
    (C) the number of levels in the organization
    (D) the time lost from work due to accidents

15. A safety officer can best secure the cooperation in a program which he is conducting if he

    (A) exercises the authority extended to him by the head of the agency
    (B) waits until a serious accident occurs to point out the necessity of a safety program
    (C) strives to become "one of the boys"
    (D) is able to convince the workers that the safety program is to their best interests

16. If a worker who is to perform a job in a hurry notices that a piece of equipment he is to use is defective he should

    (A) hold off completing the job until the equipment is either replaced or repaired
    (B) go ahead with the job because it must be completed in a hurry
    (C) consult with another subordinate
    (D) be cautious while using the defective equipment

17. A worker notices a piece of equipment which he believes can aid him in performing his work. The equipment is somewhat complicated, and he has never received any instruction as to its operation, although other employees have. He should

    (A) use the equipment because he will be able to do his work faster
    (B) put off doing his work until he has received adequate instruction in the use of the equipment
    (C) ask another worker to teach him to use the equipment
    (D) not use the equipment until he has received adequate instruction in its operation

18. If after completing an accident report you discover an additional piece of information which may influence the conclusions drawn from the report you should

    (A) ignore the information because the report has already been completed

(B) rewrite the report including the additional information you have discovered
(C) submit the original report and wait to see if the additional information is pertinent
(D) ask the injured worker if he thinks it should be included in the accident report

19. If you find that your subordinates are using improper tools while performing their functions, and if, after confronting them with this information, they tell you that requisitioning the proper tools from the tool shack is too time consuming, you should

(A) insist they use the proper tools
(B) go along with them because they have performed well in the past
(C) inform them that they will be held strictly responsible for any accidents that occur from their use of the improper tools
(D) report them to your superior

20. When a veteran worker with a clean safety record suddenly becomes involved in a series of work accidents it would be wise for the supervisor to <u>first</u>

(A) retrain the employee in safety procedures
(B) discipline the employee
(C) try to discover the cause of the accidents
(D) transfer the employee to another unit

## Explanatory Answers

1. (A) The new worker has demonstrated that he may not yet be familiar with all of the safety aspects of his duties. This is the time to give him additional training and observe how he responds.

2. (C) There is nothing in the question to make one believe this worker is a malingerer. It is reasonable for the supervisor to grant his request.

3. (B) This employee is disregarding specific instructions given to him by his supervisor. He should be disciplined immediately before he becomes involved in an accident. Once he has, it will be too late.

4. (C) The primary purpose of an accident report is to isolate the cause of the accident so that proper remedial action can be taken so that it does not occur again. Choices (A), (B), and (D) would aid in determining the cause of the accident. The

length of time the injured worker has been employed by the agency would have very little bearing.

5. (D) There is no point in delaying the correction of a subordinate who is performing his duties in an unsafe manner. He may fall victim to an accident in the meantime. The worker should be corrected immediately.

6. (C) Accident reports should be prepared promptly because the facts will still be fresh in the mind of the reporter and he will be less likely to omit important items.

7. (D) When accidents occur mostly at the end of a workday they can most likely be attributed to mental and physical fatigue on the part of the workers, especially where routine work is being performed. Perhaps more work breaks would alleviate the situation.

8. (D) Often those closest to the actual work will see things in a job the supervisor will overlook. The supervisor should always keep an open mind to suggestions from his subordinates.

9. (A) If trainees do not use the material taught them in a training session, they are probably not convinced of the value of the training material.

10. (C) It would be proper for you to talk to his supervisor first. Both the worker and the supervisor may resent any direct contact you may have with the worker because he is actually not responsible to you.

11. (D) In this situation all formalities should be abandoned. Your first action would be to render any immediate help to the victim that you can.

12. (B) If a file cabinet is loaded from the top down, it will topple forward when the top drawer is opened all the way. This is a common cause of office accidents.

13. (A) When this method is used, the stress is being equally distributed between the back and the legs.

14. (C) The number of levels in an organization would not have any bearing at all on the necessity of a safety program. The other three choices do have a bearing.

15. (D) The safety officer will be most able to secure the cooperation of the workers in an organization if he can show them how it will benefit them and how they stand to suffer if they are involved in an accident.

16. (A) The use of defective equipment is the cause of many an accident. Unfortunately, caution will not always prevent accidents if dangerous equipment is utilized.

17. (D) It is wrong for a worker to use any piece of equipment on which he has not been adequately trained. If the supervisor had wanted him to use the equipment in question, he would have seen that he was trained in its use.

18. (B) An incomplete report may become a harmful instrument.

19. (A) The supervisor should insist that his subordinates use proper tools no matter what inconveniences they may encounter in securing them. The use of improper tools has caused many an accident.

20. (C) This veteran employee has demonstrated through long service without accidents that he knows how to work safely. Obviously something is bothering him; it is the supervisor's job to discover what it is.

# ANSWER SHEET FOR READING COMPREHENSION QUIZZES

## QUIZ 1

| | | | | |
|---|---|---|---|---|
| 1 Ⓣ Ⓕ | 6 Ⓣ Ⓕ | 11 Ⓣ Ⓕ | 16 Ⓣ Ⓕ | 21 Ⓣ Ⓕ |
| 2 Ⓣ Ⓕ | 7 Ⓣ Ⓕ | 12 Ⓣ Ⓕ | 17 Ⓣ Ⓕ | 22 Ⓣ Ⓕ |
| 3 Ⓣ Ⓕ | 8 Ⓣ Ⓕ | 13 Ⓣ Ⓕ | 18 Ⓣ Ⓕ | 23 Ⓣ Ⓕ |
| 4 Ⓣ Ⓕ | 9 Ⓣ Ⓕ | 14 Ⓣ Ⓕ | 19 Ⓣ Ⓕ | 24 Ⓣ Ⓕ |
| 5 Ⓣ Ⓕ | 10 Ⓣ Ⓕ | 15 Ⓣ Ⓕ | 20 Ⓣ Ⓕ | 25 Ⓣ Ⓕ |

## QUIZ 2

| | | | | |
|---|---|---|---|---|
| 1 Ⓐ Ⓑ Ⓒ Ⓓ | 4 Ⓐ Ⓑ Ⓒ Ⓓ | 7 Ⓐ Ⓑ Ⓒ Ⓓ | 10 Ⓐ Ⓑ Ⓒ Ⓓ | 13 Ⓐ Ⓑ Ⓒ Ⓓ |
| 2 Ⓐ Ⓑ Ⓒ Ⓓ | 5 Ⓐ Ⓑ Ⓒ Ⓓ | 8 Ⓐ Ⓑ Ⓒ Ⓓ | 11 Ⓐ Ⓑ Ⓒ Ⓓ | 14 Ⓐ Ⓑ Ⓒ Ⓓ |
| 3 Ⓐ Ⓑ Ⓒ Ⓓ | 6 Ⓐ Ⓑ Ⓒ Ⓓ | 9 Ⓐ Ⓑ Ⓒ Ⓓ | 12 Ⓐ Ⓑ Ⓒ Ⓓ | 15 Ⓐ Ⓑ Ⓒ Ⓓ |

## QUIZ 3

| | | | | |
|---|---|---|---|---|
| 1 Ⓐ Ⓑ Ⓒ Ⓓ | 4 Ⓐ Ⓑ Ⓒ Ⓓ | 7 Ⓐ Ⓑ Ⓒ Ⓓ | 10 Ⓐ Ⓑ Ⓒ Ⓓ | 13 Ⓐ Ⓑ Ⓒ Ⓓ |
| 2 Ⓐ Ⓑ Ⓒ Ⓓ | 5 Ⓐ Ⓑ Ⓒ Ⓓ | 8 Ⓐ Ⓑ Ⓒ Ⓓ | 11 Ⓐ Ⓑ Ⓒ Ⓓ | 14 Ⓐ Ⓑ Ⓒ Ⓓ |
| 3 Ⓐ Ⓑ Ⓒ Ⓓ | 6 Ⓐ Ⓑ Ⓒ Ⓓ | 9 Ⓐ Ⓑ Ⓒ Ⓓ | 12 Ⓐ Ⓑ Ⓒ Ⓓ | 15 Ⓐ Ⓑ Ⓒ Ⓓ |

## QUIZ 4

| | | | | |
|---|---|---|---|---|
| 1 Ⓐ Ⓑ Ⓒ Ⓓ | 4 Ⓐ Ⓑ Ⓒ Ⓓ | 7 Ⓐ Ⓑ Ⓒ Ⓓ | 10 Ⓐ Ⓑ Ⓒ Ⓓ | 13 Ⓐ Ⓑ Ⓒ Ⓓ |
| 2 Ⓐ Ⓑ Ⓒ Ⓓ | 5 Ⓐ Ⓑ Ⓒ Ⓓ | 8 Ⓐ Ⓑ Ⓒ Ⓓ | 11 Ⓐ Ⓑ Ⓒ Ⓓ | 14 Ⓐ Ⓑ Ⓒ Ⓓ |
| 3 Ⓐ Ⓑ Ⓒ Ⓓ | 6 Ⓐ Ⓑ Ⓒ Ⓓ | 9 Ⓐ Ⓑ Ⓒ Ⓓ | 12 Ⓐ Ⓑ Ⓒ Ⓓ | 15 Ⓐ Ⓑ Ⓒ Ⓓ |

# IMPROVING YOUR READING COMPREHENSION

Whatever the test--Track Worker or Case Worker, Groundskeeper or General Clerk, Machinist or Maintenance Worker --you can increase your chances of scoring high by improving your reading comprehension skills.

Most civil service tests include some kind of reading comprehension question. It usually takes the form of a brief reading passage and one or more questions to be answered on the basis of what you have read. Sometimes the questions are statements that you must label either true or false based on the information in the reading passage. Other times the questions consist of incomplete statements followed by four choices from which you must select the one best answer. In either case, you must answer each question on the basis of what is stated in the reading passage, not upon personal opinions, prejudices or preferences.

The best way to prepare for a reading comprehension test is to practice with the kinds of questions you are likely to face. The quizzes that follow provide a variety of reading questions that will help you to develop the skill you need to score high on any reading test. Correct answers for all questions are provided at the end of the chapter.

## READING COMPREHENSION QUIZ 1

DIRECTIONS: For each question in this test, decide whether the statement is true or false based upon the information given in the reading passage.

Answer questions 1 to 4 on the basis of the information given in the following paragraph.

"Although not found in all injuries, shock is present in all serious injuries caused by accidents. While in shock, the normal activities of the body slow down. This partially explains why one of the signs of shock is pale, cold skin, since insufficient blood flows to the body parts during shock."

1. If the injury caused by an accident is serious, shock is sure to be present.

2. In shock, the heart beats faster than it normally does.

3. The face of a person suffering from shock is usually red and flushed.

4. Not enough blood goes to different parts of the body during shock.

Answer questions 5 to 8 on the basis of the information given in the following paragraph.

"Carbon monoxide is a deadly gas, the effects of which spare no one. Any person's strength will be reduced considerably by breathing this gas, even if not enough gas is taken in to overcome him or her. Wearing a handkerchief tied around the nose and mouth offers some protection against the irritating fumes of ordinary smoke, but many people have died convinced that a handkerchief will stop carbon monoxide. Any person entering a room filled with this deadly gas should wear a mask equipped with an air hose, or even better, an oxygen mask."

5. Some people feel no ill effects from carbon monoxide gas until they are overcome by it.

6. A person can die from breathing carbon monoxide gas.

7. A handkerchief tied around the nose and mouth gives some protection against the effects of ordinary smoke.

8. It is better for a person entering a room filled with carbon monoxide to wear a mask equipped with an air hose than an oxygen mask.

Your answers to questions 9 to 14 must be based only on the information given in the following paragraph and not on any other information you may have.

"Every accident should be reported even if the accident seems very unimportant. The worker involved may be unharmed, yet it is necessary in the case of all accidents to forward a written report containing all the facts that show how the accident occurred, including the time and place. The reason for this is that a situation which does not cause injury at one time may cause serious injury at another time. A written report informs the safety director of a dangerous condition and helps the investigation by supplying important facts. The safety director can therefore take steps to eliminate the hazard."

9. Only serious accidents should be reported.

10. If the worker involved in an accident is unharmed it is not necessary to send through a report.

11. An accident report should show how the accident happened and include the time and place of the accident.

12. A situation that does not cause an injury at one time cannot cause serious injury at another.

13. When a written report of an accident is made, it means that the safety director is informed of a dangerous condition.

14. The facts in an accident report do not help the safety director in the investigation of the accident.

Answer questions 15 to 19 on the basis of the information given in the following paragraph.

"Every day in New York City, 4500 miles of paved streets must be cleaned. In addition, 3000 truckloads of refuse, amounting to about 9000 tons, must be collected and disposed of. To do this job, more than 4000 pieces of motor equipment must be operated and maintained. This equipment includes 1800 trucks and over 400 pieces of snow-removal and waste-disposal equipment. Also in use are 42 barges and 4 tugboats."

15. Less than 4000 miles of paved streets must be cleaned daily in New York City.

16. On the average, each truckload of refuse amounts to about 9000 tons.

17. Of the motor equipment used, 1800 pieces are trucks.

18. For snow removal and waste disposal, over 400 pieces of equipment are used.

19. There are 42 tugboats and 4 barges in use.

Answer questions 20 to 25 on the basis of the information given in the following paragraph.

"A thorough watering of a lawn once a week during dry weather is of much greater value than daily sprinklings. If the lawn is sprinkled every day, the grass roots are less likely to grow deep in the soil, causing the plants to become weakened. In addition, weeds and fungus diseases have a better chance of growing and crowding out the grass. The best way to apply water is in the form of a fine spray which will fall gently and evenly on the surface. It is important to apply the water only as fast as the soil can take it in. If the water is applied too quickly or in a heavy spray, the surface may become so muddy that it keeps the water from seeping down into the earth. In order that the grass roots may get the greatest benefit, the water should seep down at least 4 to 6 inches into the soil."

20. Daily sprinklings of a lawn during dry weather are of less value than a thorough weekly watering.

21. When grass roots grow deep in the soil, the plants are weakened.

22. Weeds have a better chance of growing when a lawn is watered once a week.

23. A fine spray that falls gently and evenly is the best way to apply water to a lawn.

24. It is important to apply the water to a lawn very quickly.

25. A muddy surface may keep the water from going down into the earth.

# READING COMPREHENSION QUIZ 2

DIRECTIONS: In this test each reading passage is followed by an incomplete statement or a question. You are to read the paragraph and select the one of the four lettered choices which best completes the statement or answers the question.

1. In a pole-vaulting competition, the judge decides on the minimum height to be jumped. The vaulter may attempt to jump any height above the minimum. Using flexible fiberglass poles, vaulters have jumped as high as 18 feet 8¼ inches.

   According to the passage, pole vaulters

   (A) may attempt to jump any height in competition
   (B) must jump higher than 18'8¼" to win
   (C) must jump higher than the height set by the judge
   (D) must use fiberglass poles

2. Only about one-tenth of an iceberg is visible above the water. Eight to nine times as much ice is hiding below the water line. In the Antarctic Ocean, near the South Pole, there are icebergs that rise as high as 300 feet above the water.

   Icebergs in the Antarctic Ocean

   (A) are usually 300 feet high
   (B) can be as much as 3000 feet high
   (C) are difficult to spot
   (D) are a hazard to navigation

3. You can tell a frog from a toad by its skin. In general, a frog's skin is moist, smooth and shiny while a toad's skin is dry, dull and rough or covered with warts. Frogs are also better at jumping than toads are.

   You can recognize a toad by its

   (A) great jumping ability
   (B) smooth, shiny skin
   (C) lack of warts
   (D) dry, rough skin

4. Thomas Edison was responsible for over 1000 inventions in his 84-year life span. Among the most famous of his inventions are the phonograph, the electric light bulb, motion picture film, the electric generator and the battery.

   According to the passage, Thomas Edison

   (A) was the most famous inventor
   (B) was responsible for 84 inventions
   (C) invented many things in his short life
   (D) was responsible for the phonograph and motion picture film

5. Amateur sportsmen or sportswomen are those who take part in sports purely for enjoyment, not for financial reward. Professionals are people who are paid to participate in sports. Only amateurs are allowed to compete in the Olympic Games.

   One example of an amateur in sports might be

   (A) an Olympic champion
   (B) a member of the Dallas Cowboys
   (C) the holder of the heavyweight boxing crown
   (D) a participant in the World Series

6. A year--the time it takes the Earth to go exactly once around the Sun--is not 365 days. It is actually 365 days 6 hours 9 minutes 9½ seconds, or 365¼ days. Leap years make up for this discrepancy by adding an extra day once every four years.

   The purpose of leap year is to

   (A) adjust for the fact that it takes 365¼ days for the Earth to circle the sun
   (B) make up for time lost in the work year
   (C) occur every four years
   (D) allow for differences in the length of a year in each time zone

7. Scientists are taking a closer look at the recent boom in the use of wood for heating. Wood burning, it seems, releases high levels of pollutants. It is believed that burning wood produces a thousand times more CO, carbon monoxide, than natural gas does when it burns.

   According to the passage, CO is

   (A) natural gas
   (B) wood
   (C) carbon monoxide
   (D) heat

8. The average American family makes a major move every ten years. This means that family history becomes scattered. In some cases, a person searching for his family's past must hire a professional researcher to track down his ancestors.

   According to the passage, every few years

   (A) somebody tries to trace his family's history
   (B) the average American family moves
   (C) family history becomes scattered
   (D) professional researchers are hired to track down ancestors

9. When gas is leaking, any spark or sudden flame can ignite it. This can create a "flashback," which burns off the gas in a quick puff of smoke and flame. But the real danger is in a large leak, which can cause an explosion.

   According to the passage, the real danger from leaking gas is

   (A) a flashback
   (B) a puff of smoke and flame
   (C) an explosion
   (D) a spark

10. With the exception of Earth, all of the planets in our solar system are named for gods and goddesses in Greek or Roman legends. This is because the other planets were thought to be in heaven like the gods and our planet lay beneath, like the earth.

    All the planets except Earth

    (A) were part of Greek and Roman legends
    (B) were thought to be in heaven
    (C) are part of the entire solar system
    (D) were worshipped as gods

11. The Supreme Court was established by Article 3 of the Constitution. Since 1869 it has been made up of nine members--the chief justice and eight associate justices--who are appointed for life. Supreme Court justices are named by the President and must be confirmed by the Senate.

    The Supreme Court

    (A) was established in 1869
    (B) consists of nine justices

(C) consists of justices appointed by the Senate
(D) changes with each Presidential election

12. The sport of automobile racing originated in France in 1894. There are five basic types of competition: (1) the grand prix, a series of races that leads to a world championship; (2) stock car racing, which uses specially equipped standard cars; (3) midget car racing; (4) sports car racing and (5) drag racing. The best known U.S. race is the Indianapolis 500, first held in 1911.

The sport of auto racing

(A) started with the Indianapolis 500 in 1911
(B) uses only stardard cars, which are specially equipped
(C) holds its championship race in France
(D) includes five different types of competition

13. The brain controls both voluntary behavior, such as walking and thinking, and most involuntary behavior, such as the beating of the heart and breathing. In higher animals, the brain is also the site of emotions, memory, self-awareness and thought.

In higher animals, the brain controls

(A) emotions, memory and thought
(B) voluntary behavior
(C) most involuntary behavior
(D) all of the above

14. The speed of a boat is measured in knots. One knot is equal to a speed of one nautical mile an hour. A nautical mile is equal to 6080 feet, while an ordinary mile is 5280 feet.

According to the passage, which of the following statements is true?

(A) A nautical mile is longer than an ordinary mile.
(B) A speed of 2 knots is the same as 2 miles an hour.
(C) A knot is the same as a mile.
(D) The distance a boat travels is measured in knots.

15. There are only two grooves on a record--one on each side. The groove is cut in a spiral on the surface of the record. For stereophonic sound, a different sound is recorded in each wall of the groove.

The pickup produces two signals, one of which goes to the left-hand speaker and one to the right-hand speaker.

Stereophonic sound is produced by

(A) cutting extra grooves in a record
(B) recording different sounds in each wall of the groove
(C) sending the sound to two speakers
(D) having left- and right-hand speakers

# READING COMPREHENSION QUIZ 3

DIRECTIONS: In this test, each reading passage is followed by an incomplete statement or a question. You are to read the passage and select the one of the four lettered choices which best completes the statement or answers the question.

1. Many TV commercials insult our intelligence. No matter whether the product is toothpaste or aspirin, it's sure to have a "combination of medically proven and tested ingredients." Are we supposed to accept the word of athletes or rock stars as proof of the quality of a soft drink?

   This paragraph best supports the statement that

   (A) all commercials are simpleminded
   (B) many TV advertisements are an insult to our intelligence
   (C) the medical profession approves all TV commercials
   (D) athletes and rock stars do not always tell the truth

2. Many people think that only older men who have a great deal of experience should hold public office. These people lose sight of an important fact. Many of the founding fathers of our country were comparatively young men. Today more than ever our country needs young, idealistic politicians.

   The best interpretation of what this author believes is that

   (A) only experienced men should hold public office
   (B) only idealistic men should hold public office
   (C) younger men can and should take part in politics
   (D) young people don't like politics

3. According to Congressman X, "Too much of our taxpayers' money is spent on the rehabilitation of drug addicts. This is no way to solve the problem. Most of the people who spend time in rehabilitation centers go right back to taking narcotics after they leave. Instead of wasting money on rehabilitation, we should be using it to get rid of the drug peddlers."

   Congressman X implies that the way to solve the problem of drug addiction is to

(A) create more rehabilitation centers
(B) eliminate the source of the drugs
(C) put drug addicts in jail
(D) tax drug peddlers

4. It's dangerous to change the weather and the climate. We do not know enough about how such changes will affect the earth. What may seem good for one area may be bad for another. If you change a grassland into a vegetable farm, where will the cattle in that area graze? Before we tinker with our natural environment, we should be very sure of what we are doing.

The implication of this statement is that the writer believes

(A) changes in climate and weather may be harmful
(B) changing climate and weather will improve the earth's surface
(C) man should never meddle with his natural environment
(D) it's easy to figure out what will happen when you change the weather

5. The United States should be grateful to the early Portuguese sailors who, five centuries ago, began to explore unknown continents. Their explorations led to the discovery of the "New World." The first of these sailors was the Portuguese Prince Henry (1394-1460), better known as "the Navigator." As the father of maritime exploration, Prince Henry sent out expeditions of men who discovered what we know as the Gold Coast of Africa.

The sentence that best summarizes this paragraph is:

(A) America owes much to the Portuguese who laid the groundwork for the discovery of our country.
(B) Prince Henry was the father of maritime exploration.
(C) Portugal was the only country that made important discoveries in the new world.
(D) Portuguese sailors reached America long before Columbus.

6. The indiscriminate or continual use of any drug without medical supervision is dangerous. Even drugs considered harmless may result in chronic poisoning if used for a period of years. Prescriptions should not be refilled without consulting your doctor. He prescribed a given amount because he wished to limit your use of the drug to a certain time. Never use a drug

prescribed for someone else just because your symptoms appear similar. There may be differences, apparent to an expert but hidden from you, which indicate an entirely different ailment requiring different medication.

The paragraph best supports the statement that

(A) the use of drugs is very dangerous
(B) if a physician prescribes a drug it is safe to refill the prescription
(C) people with similar symptoms are usually suffering from the same ailment
(D) a drug considered harmless may be dangerous if taken over a long period of time without supervision

7. Although rural crime reporting is spottier and less efficient than city and town reporting, sufficient data is collected to support the statement that rural crime rates are lower than those in urban communities.

The paragraph best supports the statement that

(A) better reporting of crime occurs in rural areas than in cities
(B) there appears to be a lower proportion of crime in rural areas than in cities
(C) cities have more crime than towns
(D) no conclusions can be drawn regarding crime in rural areas because of inadequate reporting

8. Telegrams should be clear, concise, and brief. Omit all unnecessary words. The parts of speech most often used in telegrams are nouns, verbs, adjectives, and adverbs. If possible, do without pronouns, prepositions, articles, and copulative verbs. Use simple sentences, instead of complex and compound ones.

In writing telegrams one should always use

(A) common and simple words
(B) only nouns, verbs, adjectives, and adverbs
(C) incomplete sentences
(D) only words essential to the meaning

9. Economy once in a while is just not enough. I expect to find it at every level of responsibility, from cabinet member to the newest and youngest recruit. Controlling waste is something like bailing a boat; you have to keep at it. I have no intention of easing up on my insistence on getting a dollar of value for each dollar we spend.

The paragraph best supports the statement that

(A) we need not be concerned about items which cost less than a dollar
(B) it is advisable to buy the cheaper of two items
(C) the responsibility of economy is greater at high levels than at low levels
(D) economy is a continuing responsibility

10. The federal investigator must direct his whole effort toward success in his work. If he wishes to succeed in each investigation, his work will be by no means easy, smooth, or peaceful; on the contrary, he will have to devote himself completely and continuously to a task that requires all his ability.

An investigator's success depends most upon

(A) ambition to advance rapidly in the service
(B) persistence in the face of difficulty
(C) training and experience
(D) willingness to obey orders without delay

11. Salt has always been important in our diet as a flavoring for food, but recently doctors have come to recognize it as an absolute necessity. Most living things contain salt, and it is almost impossible to eat a normal diet without getting some. However, that "some" may not be enough. Now doctors recommend that those who normally use little salt should step up their salt consumption in hot weather, when more than usual salt intake is required.

The paragraph best supports the statement that

(A) salt is necessary if flavor is to be maintained
(B) people living on a normal diet have an intake of salt sufficient to maintain good blood pressure
(C) the body needs more salt in summer than in winter
(D) all organic life contains salt in one form or another

12. Iron is used in making our bridges and skyscrapers, subways and steamships, railroads and automobiles, and nearly all kinds of machinery--besides millions of small articles, from the farmer's scythe to the tailor's needle.

The paragraph best supports the statement that iron

(A) is the most abundant of the metals
(B) has many different uses
(C) is the strongest of all metals

(D) is the only material used in building skyscrapers and bridges

13. The labor required to produce a bushel of wheat in 1830 was three hours. Today it takes less than ten minutes. Further, it has been estimated that fifty men, employing modern farm machinery and agricultural methods, can do the work of five hundred peasants toiling under the conditions of the eighteenth century.

On the basis of the facts presented in the paragraph, one could best conclude that

(A) the increase of efficiency in agriculture is almost as great as that in manufacturing
(B) modern farm machinery has resulted in serious unemployment among farmers
(C) more than 18 times as much wheat is produced today than in 1830
(D) modern farm machinery is labor-saving

14. In the business districts of cities, collections from street letter boxes are made at stated hours, and collectors are required to observe these hours exactly. Anyone using these boxes can rely with certainty upon the time of the next collection.

The paragraph best supports the statement that

(A) mail collections in business districts are more frequent during the day than at night
(B) mail collectors are required to observe safety regulations exactly
(C) mail collections are made more often in business districts
(D) mail is collected in business districts on a regular schedule

15. Certain chemical changes, such as fermentation, are due to the action of innumerable living microorganisms known as bacteria. Bacteria also cause the decomposition of sewage.

Certain chemical changes are due to

(A) bacteria
(B) oxidation
(C) fermentation
(D) decomposition

# READING COMPREHENSION QUIZ 4

DIRECTIONS: Each selection is followed by a number of questions based upon the information given in the selection. Read the selection carefully; then read each question carefully before selecting your answer.

Answer questions 1 and 2 on the basis of the information given in the following paragraph.

"Many experiments have been made on the effects of alcoholic beverages. These studies show that alcohol decreases alertness and efficiency. It decreases self-consciousness, and at the same time increases confidence and feelings of ease and relaxation. It impairs attention and judgment. It destroys fear of consequences. Usual cautions are thrown to the winds. Habit systems become disorganized. The driver who uses alcohol tends to disregard his usual safety practices. He may not even be aware that he is disregarding them. His reaction time slows down; normally quick reactions are not possible. To make matters worse, he may not realize he is slower. His eye muscles may be so affected that his vision is not normal. He cannot correctly judge the speed of his car or of any other car. He cannot correctly estimate distances being covered by each. He becomes a highway menace."

1. The paragraph states that the drinking of alcohol makes a driver

   (A) more alert
   (B) less confident
   (C) more efficient
   (D) less attentive

2. From the above paragraph, it is reasonable to assume that a driver may overcome the bad effects of drinking alcohol by

   (A) being more cautious
   (B) relying on his good driving habits to a greater extent than normally
   (C) watching the road more carefully
   (D) waiting for the alcohol to wear off before driving

Answer questions 3 and 4 on the basis of the information given in the following paragraph.

"The racketeer is primarily concerned with business affairs, legitimate or otherwise, and preferably those that are close to the margin of legitimacy. He gets his best opportunities from business organizations that meet the need of large sections of the public for goods or services that are defined as illegitimate by the same public, such as prostitution, gambling, illicit drugs or liquor. In contrast to the thief, the racketeer and the establishments he controls deliver goods and services for money received."

3. From the above paragraph it can be deduced that suppression of racketeers is difficult because

   (A) victims of racketeers are not guilty of violating the law.
   (B) racketeers are generally engaged in fully legitimate enterprises
   (C) many people want services which are not obtainable through legitimate sources
   (D) the racketeers are well organized

4. According to the above paragraph, racketeering, unlike theft, involves

   (A) objects of value
   (B) payment for goods received
   (C) organized gangs
   (D) public approval

Answer questions 5 to 8 on the basis of the information given in the following paragraph.

ACCIDENT PREVENTION

"Many accidents and injuries can be prevented if employees learn to be more careful. The wearing of shoes with thin or badly worn soles or open toes can easily lead to foot injuries from tacks, nails, and chair and desk legs. Loose or torn clothing should not be worn near moving machinery. This is especially true of neckties, which can very easily become caught in the machine. You should not place objects so that they block or partly block hallways, corridors or other passageways. Even when they are stored in the proper place, tools, supplies and equipment should be carefully placed or piled so as neither to fall nor have anything stick out from a pile. Before cabinets, lockers or ladders are moved, the tops should be cleared of anything that might injure someone or fall off. If necessary, use a dolly to move these or other bulky objects.

"Despite all efforts to avoid accidents and injuries, though, some will happen. If an employee is injured, no matter how small the injury, he should report it to his supervisor and have the injury treated. A small cut not attended to can easily become infected, and can cause more trouble than some injuries that at first seem more serious. It never pays to take chances."

5. According to the above passage, the one statement that is not true is that

   (A) by being more careful, employees can reduce the number of accidents
   (B) women should wear shoes with open toes for comfort when working
   (C) supplies should be piled so that nothing is sticking out from the pile
   (D) if an employee sprains his wrist at work he should tell his supervisor about it

6. According to the above passage, you should not wear loose clothing when you are

   (A) in a corridor
   (B) storing tools
   (C) opening cabinets
   (D) near moving machinery

7. According to the above passage, before moving a ladder you should

   (A) test all the rungs
   (B) get a dolly to carry the ladder at all times
   (C) remove everything from the top of the ladder which might fall off
   (D) remove your necktie

8. According to the above passage, an employee who gets a slight cut should

   (A) have it treated to help prevent infection
   (B) know that a slight cut becomes more easily infected than a big cut
   (C) pay no attention to it as it can't become serious
   (D) realize that it is more serious than any other type of injury

Answer questions 9 to 13 on the basis of the information given in the following paragraph.

INSTRUCTIONS REGARDING UNUSUAL OCCURRENCES

A prompt report of every unusual occurrence will be made by telephone to the Station Supervisor's office, whether or not a written report is used. The telephone report should include the time, place, and a concise statement of the circumstances and action taken, including the names and addresses of passengers and the names and badge numbers of all employees and police officers involved. Details will be confirmed in a written report when requested. No unusual occurrence is too trivial to report.

If the occurrence is of an emergency nature, or one which cannot be handled by the station personnel, the Transit Police will be notified first and the Station Supervisor's office immediately thereafter.

Train whistle signals for help (one long, one short, one long and one short blasts of the whistle) will be given immediate response by station section employees.

9. When reporting an unusual occurrence, a railroad clerk need not say

   (A) where it happened
   (B) what was done about it
   (C) when it occurred
   (D) why it happened

10. A telephone report of an unusual occurrence should be made by a railroad clerk

   (A) if no police are present
   (B) only if the occurrence is serious
   (C) in every case
   (D) according to his judgment

11. A railroad clerk must submit a written report of an unusual occurrence

   (A) so that the supervisor's office need not take the telephone message in writing
   (B) if the telephone report would be too long
   (C) to prove that the incident occurred
   (D) if it is requested

12. A telephone report is most clearly required from a railroad clerk who observes

   (A) an exasperated passenger violently try to shake a vending machine
   (B) a passenger fall on a station stairway
   (C) two passengers arguing about pushing
   (D) that car doors on a train are slow in closing

13. A train crew wishing help from station section em-

ployees must

(A) use a whistle signal only
(B) blow the whistle for an appreciable time
(C) blow a specified whistle signal
(D) use a special whistle carried by the crew

Answer questions 14 and 15 on the basis of the information given in the following paragraphs.

"The work goals of an agency can best be reached if the employees understand and agree with these goals. One way to gain such understanding and agreement is for management to encourage and seriously consider suggestions from employees in the setting of agency goals."

14. On the basis of the paragraph above, the best way to achieve the work goals of an agency is to

(A) make certain that employees work as hard as possible
(B) study the organizational structure of the agency
(C) encourage employees to think seriously about the agency's problems
(D) stimulate employee understanding of the work goals

15. On the basis of the paragraph above, understanding of and agreement with agency goals can be gained by

(A) allowing the employees to set agency goals
(B) reaching agency goals quickly
(C) legislative review of agency operations
(D) employee participation in setting agency goals

# Answer Key

## QUIZ 1

| | | | | |
|---|---|---|---|---|
| 1. T | 6. T | 11. T | 16. F | 21. F |
| 2. F | 7. T | 12. F | 17. T | 22. F |
| 3. F | 8. F | 13. T | 18. T | 23. T |
| 4. T | 9. F | 14. F | 19. F | 24. F |
| 5. F | 10. F | 15. F | 20. T | 25. T |

## QUIZ 2

| | | | | |
|---|---|---|---|---|
| 1. C | 4. D | 7. C | 10. B | 13. D |
| 2. B | 5. A | 8. B | 11. B | 14. A |
| 3. D | 6. A | 9. C | 12. D | 15. B |

## QUIZ 3

| | | | | |
|---|---|---|---|---|
| 1. B | 4. A | 7. B | 10. B | 13. D |
| 2. C | 5. A | 8. D | 11. C | 14. D |
| 3. B | 6. D | 9. D | 12. B | 15. A |

## QUIZ 4

| | | | | |
|---|---|---|---|---|
| 1. D | 4. B | 7. C | 10. C | 13. C |
| 2. D | 5. B | 8. A | 11. D | 14. D |
| 3. C | 6. D | 9. D | 12. B | 15. D |